Your Book,
Your Way

Your Book, Your Way

How to Choose the Best Publishing Option for Your Book, Your Wallet and Yourself

Sonja Hakala

Full Circle Press

www.FullCirclePress.com

Copyright

Your Book, Your Way:
How to Choose the Best Publishing Option for Your Book,
Your Wallet and Yourself

Sonja Hakala

Published 2011 by Full Circle Press LLC

Cover and interior design by Sonja Hakala

Full Circle Press LLC
PO Box 71
West Hartford, VT 05084

www.SonjaHakala.com

ISBN: 978-0-9790046-1-2

Table of Contents

 Dedication

In 2000, Stephen King became the first major author to release a book only in an electronic format. The day *Riding the Bullet* was released, over 400,000 eager readers crashed the servers as they downloaded copies of his novella.

In 2011, author Barry Eisler (*Rain Fall, Inside Out*) turned down a contract offer for $500,000 in order to publish his own books because he felt he would make more money as well as get his work into print faster than with a traditional publisher.

Today, more than 25 percent of the best-selling books on Amazon.com are independently published by their authors.

For over 500 years, writers could not get their work into readers' hands without the help of publishers. That world has changed forever.

This book is dedicated to all of you—the publishing pioneers to come. Go ahead, you can do this.

This book would not be possible if it were not for the support of my husband, Jay Davis. I am truly grateful in every way.

I would also like to acknowledge the work of my priceless editor, Ruth Sylvester. I've trusted her with my work for years, and I'm glad she's by my side. I'd also like to thank photographer Jim Block for helping me understand the right way to handle images.

Coming Full Circle

A FEW YEARS AGO, I was at a dinner party with an author who had received a sizable advance for her first book, a six-figure sizable advance. But by the time of the dinner party, her first novel was long past, and she was struggling with her second book. Not writing it but getting it published.

She told me that her agency, a large one in New York, required all of its clients to have their work edited before they considered submitting it to a publisher. So the author did that, with an editor recommended by her agency.

"I don't think that editor liked one word of my book. She said it wouldn't sell enough," the author said. "There was a time when publishers took on works that had real merit. Now it's all money, money, money."

Like most writers, my conversational partner believed that book publishing is solely an extension of what she does, put words on paper for the edification of others. But here's the truth. Book publishing was created by venture capitalists who saw profitable opportunities in the manufacturing and sale of finished products (books) from raw materials (manuscripts). Like every other risk-prone financial venture, sometimes the risk pays off. Sometimes it doesn't.

For more than five centuries, book publishers have occupied a place in the middle between printers and booksellers. Because of its position in this three-way relationship, the book publishing industry has always been far more responsive to developments in printing and the demands of booksellers than to the needs of writers.

The process we now refer to as traditional publishing solidified in the late 19th century, about the time Charles Dickens, Mark Twain, and Edith Wharton were publishing their work. But over the past two decades, the structure of traditional publishing has been torn apart by digital print technology, electronic books and reading devices, and the internet. In other words, you no longer need a publisher to get your work to readers. Now you can publish, print or digitize, and sell your own books, keeping the profit for yourself.

In many ways, book publishing has come full circle, back to the roots of the industry as it was practiced in Europe before Johannes Gutenberg perfected a system for the mass printing of books. Before Gutenberg, anyone who wanted to write a book had to do it all, making copies one at a time with ink and parchment while managing their own distribution and sales. After Gutenberg, authors gained the capacity to reach larger audiences because books could be printed in vast quantities. But they lost control over the manufacturing, distribution, and sale of their work.

To a large extent, authors have regained that control without losing access to the means of mass producing and selling their work.

But as Sargeant Phil Esterhaus used to say on *Hill Street Blues*, "be careful out there." The ground-shaking changes wrought in the book publishing industry by technology have also spawned a number of companies that are, shall we say, less than scrupulous about the promises they make and keep with authors. What was once considered "a gentleman's profession" with well-known standards of quality has now become a confusing jungle of claims, counter claims, and rules that seem to change daily. As a result, too many folks are spending too much money on unnecessary services in order to see their work in print.

As every writer can attest, finishing a manuscript is a monumental task. It's also a profound emotional experience as well as the achievement of a dream. When writers decide to publish, this potent emotional mix makes them vulnerable at precisely the moment when they need to be at their most hardheaded.

Why? Because book publishing—whether you do it independently or seek the support of a traditional company—is a business venture, pure and simple. While your work is personal and precious to you, traditional book publishers view it as a sales opportunity. And this is equally true of firms that market themselves as self-publishing companies.

How do you make good publishing decisions for your work? By learning how to think like a publisher. That's what *Your Book, Your Way* is all about: How to understand the industry from the inside out, how to separate genuine opportunities from the snake oil, how to determine what your book needs, and how to get it.

In the early 1990s, I was a writer and book designer who started freelancing because the book publisher I worked for had been sold to a company based in New York City, a fact that made most of its Vermont staff "redundant." But my name was obviously active on the local word-of-mouth network because I started receiving telephone calls from folks I didn't know that began with the words: "A friend of mine told me you know how to publish books."

Some of the callers were people who wanted advice about query letters or finding an agent. But a noticeable number came from published authors who had had their dreams smashed to bits because getting published had fallen far short of their expectations. I recall in particular one sobbing author who could not find a publisher for her second novel because she had failed to earn back the advance on her first book. As I explained why that mattered so much, she cried "Why doesn't somebody tell you these things before you get into publishing?"

Nowadays, she wouldn't cry. She'd get out there and independently publish her own book, on paper and electronically.

So can you. In these pages, I talk a lot about paths to publishing, about the advantages and disadvantages of each, and what considerations are important in each choice. My goal is to put the information you need in your hands so that you make the right decision for your book and pocketbook.

There are five main paths to publishing: Independently publishing your own work and making it available for sale to the public; publishing privately just for family and friends; using a company that provides author services to self-publish your book; partnering with a traditional publisher who takes on the financial risk of producing your book; and electronic publishing.

Which path is right for you and your work? That's what we're here to find out.

You're welcome to visit my website any time at www.SonjaHakala.com, and when you do publish your book, please write and tell me about your journey. I'd really like to know how it turns out.

Sonja Hakala
Sonja@FullCirclePress.com

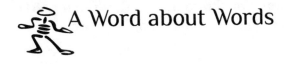A Word about Words

AS AN INDUSTRY, book publishing is more than 500 years old. No one planned how the industry would develop, and consequently it has a lot of moving parts.

In the language common among publishers, there's a bewildering (to the newcomer, at least) mixture of old and new words and concepts. For example, words that refer to the different parts of a book such as front matter, back matter, and text block all harken back to the time of Gutenberg and letterpress printing. When we refer to en dashes and em dashes or uppercase letters and lowercase, we're using terms that are hundreds of years old.

Industry-wide terms such as wholesaler and distributor are now used interchangeably but not too long ago, they were distinct entities. I often hear writers use the words marketing and sales as if they meant the same thing. They don't, and it's a wise author or publisher who knows the difference.

Whenever I use a bit of publishing speak for the first time, I'll define the term. But if you jump around in these pages, you might miss that. That's why there's a big, fat glossary of terms at the back of this book. When you come across a word that doesn't quite make sense or a term that seems crucial for your understanding, I recommend that you flip to the back of the book so we don't lose you along the way.

IN ADDITION

In addition to this book, you are welcome to visit my website at www.SonjaHakala.com. There are free PDFs there for you to download—examples of press releases, a short tutorial on how to storyboard a book, examples of postcards created for marketing books—and more. Just follow the links from the info page for *Your Book, Your Way.*

Also note that my company, Full Circle Press LLC, provides book counseling and author services such as editing and book design for authors who decide to publish their work independently. There's more information on my website, www.SonjaHakala.com, and you're welcome to email me anytime at: Sonja@FullCirclePress.com.

CHAPTER ONE

Book Publishing and How It Grew

IT'S TEMPTING TO PAY attention to what titles are selling well on Amazon or get to the top of the *New York Times* bestseller list, and believe you understand what drives the book publishing industry. To an outsider, it seems that publishers operate with a herd mentality, that if books about a boy wizard named Harry Potter are selling well then readers want more books about boy wizards so that's what publishers buy.

After all, it's readers' tastes that dictate what happens in book publishing, right?

Well, that's true in the short term. But close observation of book publishing as an industry reveals that bestseller lists have less to do with what a publisher buys from an author than you would think.

The book publishing industry developed in the quintessential middle ground between those who produce the raw materials of a book (writers and their manuscripts) and those who manufacture finished products from those raw materials (printers and their printing presses).

When you study the history of the book publishing industry, you'll realize its internal structure has always been dictated by the technology of printing. To put this in a contemporary perspective, the chaos in contemporary book publishing was not caused by changes among writers or new demands from readers or booksellers. Nope, publishing as we've known it from the mid-19th century to today is coming apart at the seams because of digital printing.

To understand the full scope of this change and what it means for you, give me a few moments of your time to understand the history of printing.

GUTENBERG, JOHANNES: PRINTER

In 1439, in Germany, a clever goldsmith named Johannes Gutenberg got involved in a secret operation that included a wine press, ink, oil, paper, various metals, and a device to mold letters one at a time. The result of this man's secret operation is credited with changing the course of history in western Europe, changes that eventually touched every corner of the world.

When you say the name Gutenberg, everyone thinks "Oh, the movable-type guy." But crediting Gutenberg with merely inventing movable type is actually an injustice. What Gutenberg really invented was a complete printing system.

Think about what you need to write a letter by hand—a writing implement (pencil or pen) that holds a substance (ink or graphite) with which you can make a mark on a surface (paper) that can be read by someone else. At each step in this process, these objects—the pen, the ink, the paper—must work together in a very explicit way so that you can write a letter and someone else can read it. But what would you do if you didn't have ink that flowed easily or only a paper towel to write on? What if you wanted to print hundreds of copies of your letter? What would you do? These are the challenges that Gutenberg faced.

Let's define movable type before we go much further. When you use movable type, you create swaths of text by combining hundreds of individual metal components—letters, numerals, spaces, punctuation marks—so they function as a single unit. The beauty of movable type is that when your printing job is done, you can take all those individual components apart and reconfigure them in a new block of text.

Compare this type of printing to a rubber stamp. With a rubber stamp, every letter, space and punctuation mark is fixed, to be used in one configuration only. You can see the advantages of movable type, I'm sure.

The concept of movable type was well-known in Europe by the time of Gutenberg. It was developed and used in different parts of Asia—primarily China and Korea—in the 11th century. The Asian versions of movable type were made of ceramic, wood, and metal. But the pictograph alphabets of Asia made mass production of text a cumbersome process because there were so many letters. Compare this scenario with the one Gutenberg faced—26 letters, ten numerals, and a handful of common punctuation marks.

Since Gutenberg was a goldsmith by profession, the choice of using metal to create letters that could be used again and again must have been obvious. Metal stands up well to being inked and pressed on paper. When it gets worn, you can melt it and reuse it. But you need the right combination of metals to make type that leaves a clear impression on paper without punching holes in its surface. To solve this problem, Gutenberg mixed lead, tin, and antimony for his type. This combination is still in use in letterpress printing today.

At the time Gutenberg began his work, ink was simply a mixture of colorant in water, and the quality of paper was haphazard at best. So Gutenberg developed an oil-based ink that dried on the surface of paper without blurring or soaking in. And he developed a way to make paper with a consistent finish to hold just the right amount of ink.

Of all his inventions, Gutenberg's matrix molding system for creating metal copies of the same letter over and over again was the most significant. Imagine the time it would take to individually carve every letter e on this page!

As far removed as it may seem, you are holding an object that uses the discoveries Gutenberg made so many years ago. For example, the paper that this is printed on has a finish made expressly to hold the type of ink used in the machine that printed it.

Whole books have been penned about Gutenberg, and the impact of his incredible printing machine. Many historians consider his contribution to the culture of western Europe the triggering mechanism for what became the Renaissance. Why? Because there were more books to read.

It's estimated that the number of volumes present in Europe at the time of Gutenberg's invention was five thousand. That's all copies of all books of all kinds in all of western Europe. Fifty years after the printing press's introduction, the number of volumes had grown to five million.

More books created a need for more readers. More readers created a need for more education, teachers, schools, paper and papermakers, inks, glue for binding, and so on. Before the political and religious power structures in Europe knew what hit them, superstition was replaced by knowledge, and the various cultures of Western Europe were out of the Middle Ages and into the Age of Reason.

Amazing what a little paper and ink will do, isn't it?

But there's one fundamental change in the history of printing that often gets overlooked. Writers, the producers of the raw material that gets made into books, lost control of their work to Gutenberg's invention. While they welcomed the opportunity to make multiple copies of their work quickly and easily, the expense of doing so was beyond the reach of all but the wealthiest writers. (Always a small minority, at best.) After Gutenberg, the power to publish moved to printers and from there to a new class of entrepreneurs we call publishers.

THE PRINT-RUN RULE

The photograph on the next page is of a composing stick that I filled with letters, punctuation marks, and spacers. I know it's impossible to read because the letters are set in mirror-image fashion so let me interpret. It says:

"This is an example of a short paragraph that has been typeset by hand. It will be printed on a hand platen press. Each letter in this short piece is an individual bit of metal. It took almost two hours to do this."

This is a composing stick filled with letters and spacers.
This device is used with a letterpress printer.
Selecting and placing text in a composing stick is
commonly referred to as setup or composition.

Believe it or not, this device is the origin of the book publishing industry as we knew it B. D. (Before Digital). In printing, the time it takes for a typesetter (also called a compositor) to pick out the right letters, numbers, spaces and punctuation marks is called "setup" or "composition."

Setup, whether it's for a letterpress or an offset press (the current technology of choice for producing large numbers of books) takes time, more time than printing. Once this part of the printing process is done, you can make as many copies of a text as you please with little effort or expense.

But there's a caveat—the cost of setup for letterpress or offset printing is the same no matter how many copies of a book you print. In other words, the cost of setup makes it economically impractical to print just one copy of a book because the cost of that book would be prohibitively expensive (in the thousands of dollars).

In fact, the minimum number of copies to print under this scenario is somewhere in the neighborhood of one thousand. At that point, the per-copy cost of a book becomes small enough to ensure a publisher's profit when their books sell.

This fact of printing life ruled the world of book publishing from the time of Gutenberg to the late 20th century when digital printing became technologically feasible and cost effective. For five centuries, this fact of printing life forced publishers to make educated guesses about how many copies of a book would sell (a print run) before they even considered offering a contract to a writer. This fact of publishing life is at the root of the relentless chase for blockbusters. It's the main reason why so many well-written and well-researched manuscripts are rejected by traditional publishers.

It is all well and good to check the bestseller lists on Amazon.com or the *New York Times* to determine contemporary reader tastes. But if you really want to see the future of the book publishing industry, pay attention to what's happening in the printing industry.

THE ADVENT OF DIGITAL PRINTING

Digital printing is the technology that allows you to make copies of anything you wish from your computer. It is the same technology that drives copying machines and scanners. And it's part and parcel of all digital cameras.

Yeah, it's everywhere. In fact, it's difficult to remember a time when you couldn't make a copy of anything you chose just by laying the original on a glass screen and pushing a button. But sentient beings born before 1960 can tell you stories about mimeograph machines with their smelly purple ink or how they tucked sheets of carbon paper between pieces of white paper before rolling them into a typewriter.

I know, I know, the stuff of dinosaur legends.

The roots of digital printing actually reach as far back as 1778 when a German scientist named Georg Christoph Lichtenberg discovered the basic principles of a dry printing method called electrostatic printing. It used static electricity—the sparky stuff that makes your hair stand up on end when you pull a fleece jacket off in winter—produced by a contraption called an electrophorus. When the buildup of static was discharged near fine particulates, the result was distinct patterns.

These principles had to wait until 1938 to get a push in the right direction when an American physicist and patent attorney named Chester Carlson combined electrostatic printing with photography to create a dry printing process he called electrophotography. Carlson, in essence, invented the technology that is the basis for all copying machines.

As seems to be the norm with anything new, it took Carlson quite a while to get anyone to see the potential of his invention. In fact, it was six years before anyone took an interest in his work.

Carlson's technology was cumbersome, as are the prototypes for most inventions. But finally, in 1959, the first machines that we would recognize as copiers were introduced to the public. By this time, the name of the technology had been changed to xerography, the Greek equivalent of "dry printing". You might more readily recognize that word as part of a company created to produce copying machines, the Xerox Corporation.

Now xerography is only half of the digital printing equation. The other half, as you might suspect, is the computer. When you marry these technologies to one another, you eventually get to the printers most of us have at home. And if you put those home printers on steroids, you get very large, very fast, and very efficient digital printers that can economically print and bind a single copy of a book in less than a minute.

And here's the kicker—digital printing does not use printing plates to create copies. The setup to print digitally is within the means of anyone who owns a computer, has some technical knowledge, and some software.

In other words, with digital printing, no one needs to

figure out how many copies of a book to print based on a best guess of how many will sell. Now you can print as many copies as you want, one at a time, as needed.

At this point, the cost of digitally printing a single copy of a book is still more than the single-copy cost of a book printed by offset. But this greater expense is easily recouped. We get into the nitty gritty of this in Chapter Ten, page 99, when we talk about the math of publishing so push on!

CHAPTER TWO

Why Do You Want to Publish a Book?

BEFORE WE VENTURE down any publishing path, we need to have some idea which one will best serve your needs. In order to do that, I need to ask you some questions.

I want you to find a writing implement and turn to page 26 to record your answers to these questions. Take your time and consider your answers seriously. It's quite possible that you will refine them as we go along, and that's OK. But I want you to have a starting point as you explore options.

Let's begin with an exercise in imagination. Picture a finished book in your hands. It's your book, and you can see your name on its front cover.

You're not keeping this book. You are going to do something with it. The question is what.

Got the picture? OK, here are the first questions I'd like you to answer.

- Have you signed this book for someone who just paid money for it?

- Are you giving this book to a family member?

- Are you sending it to a reviewer?

- Are you using the book as a fundraiser for a non-profit or special event?

- Are you selling the book at a conference where you are speaking?

- Are you using the book as the text in a class you're teaching?

- Are you presenting a copy of this book to your town's historical society?

- Are you selling copies of your book as companion pieces to an exhibit of your creative work?

OK, that's a good start. Let's press ahead with one very important question:

- Do you intend to sell copies of this book or will it be used exclusively as a gift?

Both answers to this question are legitimate because a number of people want to publish books for private audiences. They may have written a memoir or a family history that's intended strictly for family members. They may want to create picture books for their children or grandchildren. They may be commemorating a significant event for a group. Or their book may be part of a giveaway in a marketing or sales strategy.

If it is your intention to give away—not sell—copies of your book, this is called private publishing, and there's a whole section devoted to economical private publishing options starting on page 119.

If you intend to sell copies of your book, this is called open publishing, and the bulk of this book is dedicated to ways in which you can make this happen. But we need to know something about where you'd like to sell your book in order to pinpoint the best option for you. Here's a few questions on that subject.

- Do you want to sell your book only on Amazon.com?

- Do you want to sell your book in bookstores as well as on Amazon?

- Do you want your book to be available in specialty stores such as those devoted to home improvement or crafts or in museums?

- Do you want to sell your book at conferences or at workshops where you speak or teach?

- Do you want to be the only one selling copies of your book?

- Do you want libraries to be able to purchase copies of your book?

Here is the last question you need to answer.

- How much money are you prepared to spend to get your book published? You don't need an exact figure but think about this for a while. What is your budget for this venture? Zero is a legitimate answer, one with built-in limitations to be sure, but legitimate all the same.

As you answer these questions, you are developing a description of your personal publishing goal. Use this goal as your guide in the following chapters in order to determine what avenue or avenues are right for your work.

Whatever your publishing goals, I urge you to read all of the options covered in these pages before making a final decision. You may discover a scenario that fits your goals better than what you originally planned.

USE THIS PAGE FOR YOUR ANSWERS

CHAPTER THREE

Paths to Publishing: An Overview

NOT TOO MANY years ago, before digital printing and online sales, there were but two options open to authors who wanted to see their work in print:

- Acceptance by a commercial publisher who paid for the editing, design, printing, and distribution of books in return for a share of the proceeds of their sale.

- Hiring what was then called a "vanity press" who was paid by an author to oversee the printing of her or his book. In return for their money, vanity press authors got hundreds of copies of their book, most of which sat in a garage or attic getting dusty because there was no way to distribute or sell them.

Nowadays, the publishing jungle positively teems with options for the ambitious author. The following is a list that's pretty close to exhaustive with a brief description of the publishing goals best served by each option.

PRIVATE PUBLISHING

While there's no hard-and-fast definition of private publishing, there are two distinguishing characteristics: The number of copies printed is small and most, if not all, of them are used as gifts. There are ways to make privately published works available for sale online but the bulk of this type of publishing is targeted to an audience known to the author. There are a number of ways to privately publish a book on your own but these are the main categories.

• HANDMADE BOOKS

The least expensive and least technical way to publish your own book is to write it by hand, on sheets of plain white paper which are copied, collated, and personally distributed. This type of private publishing is often used for a poet's first chapbook, or for short books meant as gifts for family members.

• WORD PROCESSING YOUR OWN BOOKS

If you're minimally savvy on the technology front, you can create digital files in word processing programs that can be copied and bound in book form at your local copy shop. Though books printed this way can be sold through online booksellers, this method works best for limited print runs with personal distribution.

• LETTERPRESS PRINTING

From the time of Johannes Gutenberg's printing press (1450) until offset printing became the norm in the early 1900s, the mass printing of all works on paper was done by letterpress. While not as important as it once was, letterpress printing is thriving as a artisanal craft. This type of printing works best for short books with limited print runs.

• PUBLISHING LIMITED-EDITION BOOKS ONLINE

There are several online companies that make it easy for folks to put together full-color, limited edition books with their own photographs and text. Because the printing costs for this type of publishing are high, it is recommended for special occasion publishing such as preserving family or personal history, to accompany an art exhibit or to commemorate a special event.

OPEN PUBLISHING

Works that are openly published are meant to be available for sale to the public. This type of publishing includes electronic books as well as books on paper.

When investigating your open publishing options, it is wise to pay attention to the way in which your work makes its way from you to your potential readers. This part of the process is called distribution, and how it's handled makes a great deal of difference in your sales potential.

As you may guess, most books are openly published because most authors want to share their work—and get paid for it. There are three categories of open publishing—independent publishing, self-publishing (AKA vanity publishing or print on demand), and traditional publishing.

• INDEPENDENT PUBLISHING

Independent publishers create their own companies for the purpose of publishing books on paper, electronic books or audio editions of their work. Independent publishers retain all of the rights to the works they publish, and do not share the proceeds of sales (royalties) with anyone.

The hallmark of independent publishers is their attention to quality. An independently published book is indistinguishable from anything from a traditional publisher when it sits on a bookstore's shelves whether that shelf is online or in a physical store. There is a lot to be said about independent publishing in the section starting on page 33.

• SELF–PUBLISHING
(ALSO CALLED VANITY PUBLISHING OR PRINT ON DEMAND)

The lines between some self-publishing companies and independent publishers are becoming thinner in one respect—author rights. Some self-publishing companies such as Blurb and Lulu now leave author rights where they belong—with the author. But others do not, and this difference is key.

Other than author rights, the great difference between publishing your own work independently and enlisting the aid of a self-publishing company is who does what during the publishing process, particularly for books on paper. If you hire a company to edit, design, and print your book, the quality of the book is dependent on the quality of the company you hire. And what those standards are may be unclear.

This is an area where you need to proceed with caution and a whole lot of information. To investigate this option, please turn to page 129.

WHAT DOES PRINT-ON-DEMAND REALLY MEAN?

Many folks think the term print-on-demand refers to a type of publishing. Not so. Print-on-demand is another name for digital print technology, and it's used by traditional publishers as well as independent and self-publishers. In fact, if you own a printer and a computer, you own a form of print-on-demand technology.

When you have a word processing document (or any document, really) open on your computer, and hit the keys to print, you make a demand that a copy of your document be committed to paper. This is print-on-demand. Digital book printers own machines with this same technology but on steroids. When a demand for print is made (an order is placed for a book), the whole work is printed, paginated, and bound in a cover in mere minutes.

This technology made the development of companies who sell publishing services to authors—such as iUniverse, Author House, and Trafford—possible.

Print-on-demand technology is all about printing and should never be equated with any particular form of book publishing.

• TRADITIONAL PUBLISHING

With all of the new avenues open to authors who wish to

publish their work, the industry once known simply as "book publishing" has evolved into what we now call "traditional book publishing." In traditional publishing, a company contracts with an author for certain rights to an author's work then pays to have that work edited, designed, printed, and made available for sale.

The main difference between traditional publishing and the other publishing avenues we just discussed is who pays to have a book produced. If a publisher pays all the expenses of book production in return for some or all of an author's rights to a particular work, that is traditional publishing.

• ELECTRONIC PUBLISHING

The world of digital books is changing while you read this sentence, as large companies such as Amazon and Apple jockey for the dominant position in this field. At this point in time, no one can predict for sure what technology will eventually become the norm.

But in the meantime, there are simple and inexpensive ways to publish your book electronically. There's no reason not to publish your book online as well as on paper. See the chapter on electronic publishing on page 157.

Let's begin our discussion of the paths to publication with an in-depth look at independent publishing. Much of the information in this section also pertains to the other publishing paths we'll explore.

CHAPTER FOUR

Publishing Path One: Independent Publishing

WHEN YOU CHOOSE to publish your book independently, you take on all of the tasks performed by a traditional publisher. In fact, you're going to set yourself up in business as a publishing company.

This means that the quality standards of your book are up to you, and the final product you sell to the public is a reflection not only of your writing but of your business practices. Remember, you're asking folks to spend money and time on your product. Make it worth their while so they'll recommend you to others and be willing to buy from you again.

A CHECKLIST FOR THE INDEPENDENT PUBLISHER

The following list represents the major steps that an independent publisher takes to develop a high-quality book from a raw (unedited) manuscript. Once you've digested this list, plunge into the following chapters for in-depth advice on how to publish your book independently.

1. The manuscript is edited by someone with book editing experience. One of the best ways to locate an editor with this experience is through a mid-sized, traditional publishing

company or university press. Call and ask for the editorial department then request recommendations.

2. Choose a name for your publishing company.

Check with the secretary of state's office in your state to be certain the name you choose is not already taken. If you're planning a website for your publishing company, purchase your website name now.

3. Purchase ISBN numbers online through www.ISBN.org.

Currently, the cost of a single ISBN (International Standard Book Number) is $125, and a block of ten is $250. If you think you may publish a second book or plan to publish electronically as well as on paper, purchase a block of ten ISBNs.

During the purchasing process, you will be offered the opportunity to purchase bar codes with your ISBN to use on the back cover of your book. This isn't necessary, depending on the printer you choose. Many printers provide these bar codes. If you find you need a bar code, you can purchase it at a later date.

Remember, ISBNs are assigned to publishers, not authors, which is why you need to choose a publishing company name before you take this step. Online purchase of ISBNs requires a credit card. You can purchase ISBNs through the mail but there is a fee for this service. There is also a one-time charge for setting your publishing company up with the ISBN agency.

4. Choose your printer, and printing method. This may seem like a cart-before-the-horse sequence of events but your choice of printer has an impact on many of your subsequent decisions. If your printer requires you to set up an account with them, take this step now.

For a list of book printers, please see page 79. And be sure to read Chapter Ten starting on page 99 on publishing math before you make your final choice.

5. When your copy editor returns your corrected manuscript,

make your changes right away. It is easier and less expensive to make large alterations to a text at this point in time.

6. Choose a designer for your cover and the interior of your book. This step may take some time. You can find book designers online but I would recommend taking a more local approach. Book designers often work freelance with book publishers, particularly with small to midsize publishers and university presses. Call to ask for recommendations.

Locally published magazines can sometimes be a source for recommendations as well as local non-profit organizations, associations, and colleges.

Be sure to shop around for this important service. Ask to see samples of a graphic designer's work, and be sure they have book design experience. Ask how they charge for their service. The most common is a per-hour fee that can range from $25 to $125 per hour. While that higher number may make you gasp, remember that an experienced designer may take far less time to create a cover and typeset your interior than an inexperienced designer.

7. Once a book designer is chosen, the corrected manuscript is turned over to her or him for design purposes. Once you settle on a design for your interior, the book can be typeset. See page 63 for information about interior design.

8. Working with your book designer, choose an image for your cover. Be as clear as possible with your designer about your expectations and tastes. See Chapter Six, page 47, for more information about cover design.

9. When your book is typeset for the first time, be sure to proofread it yourself and hire a professional proofreader to do the same. Your copy editor may be a good choice for this task or may be able to recommend someone who is. Local publishers can also be a good source of recommendations for a proofreader.

10. When you have settled on a front cover, write the back cover copy, and let your designer complete the cover process. Be sure your designer understands and can carry out the necessary technical tasks to create what your printer needs. Also ask your designer to create different versions of your front cover and full cover for use in marketing. You will need formats that can be used in print, on the web, and attached to emails.

11. Prepare your marketing materials and finalize your marketing plans. See Chapter Nine, page 81, for more details about this process, and some advice.

12. When your proofreader returns your typeset pages with corrections, add yours as well so that your designer can create the final version of your book's interior. When this step is complete, please look it over one more time before the printer's files are prepared. Remember, you are the final word on how your book looks and reads. No one can replace you.

13. Once the cover and interior files are prepared for the printer, your book is sent off. If a book is printed by offset, an order for a specific number of copies is made at this time. If you're printing digitally, there is no need to establish a print run because copies of your book can be made as needed.

14. A proof copy of the book is sent to you, as the publisher, for final approval. This step is done no matter the printing method. You want to be sure all of the pages are there and in the correct order, that the quality of the printing is what you expect, that the spine fits the book correctly. You may want to involve your graphic designer in this step.

15. If you decide to print by offset, once your proof is approved, your print run is completed and shipped to the warehouse of your chosen distributor or to you to await orders from customers. If you are printing digitally, your book should be ready to order once you approve your proof.

CHAPTER FIVE

Editing

THIS MAY SEEM like a strange question to ask, but what are you doing when you read this sentence? Are you looking at every letter in it? Every word? Did you notice the comma after the word *ask* or the question mark following the word *sentence*?

The act of reading is actually an act of decoding. When you think about it, the letters printed on this page are nothing more than ink strewn around in particular shapes. Language is a code. In English, our code consists of 26 letters, ten numerical symbols, and a handful of punctuation marks that function like conductors for a symphony orchestra. When we read, we don't focus on single letters nor do we see every individual word or punctuation mark unless wwweeeee sssssslllllllloooooowwwww ddddoooooowwwwwnnnnn.

In actuality, our eyes flicker about a page of type, stopping and starting on a word here, another there. In most cases, we recognize common words by their shapes, and infer a lot of the meaning of a sentence or paragraph from a small number of key words, context, and language patterns. For example, in English, we expect and do find our adjectives in front of our nouns as in "red apple." In French, adjectives arrive after the noun in a sentence as in "pomme rouge." We rely on writers, editors, and publishers to serve up our reading material in a manner that adheres to the code as we understand it.

What happens when we come across a book that doesn't adhere to these standards? Let me give you an example by telling you a story about my friend Carol.

Carol is not a writer, not an editor, not involved in the world of book publishing at all except in her capacity as a voracious reader. One day, I ran into her outside a local bookstore where she had purchased an obscure volume on an obscure topic that was of great interest to her. She was excited by her find, couldn't wait to get home and read it.

About a week later, I saw her again. "How was the book?" I asked.

She flew into a fury as only a disappointed reader can. "It was awful, full of misspellings, no captions under the pictures so you had no idea what you were looking at. The margins in the middle of the book were so small, you had to constantly tilt it to see a word. Nothing at the top of the page to tell you what the chapters were about, missing page numbers. I took it to the bookstore and got my money back."

Carol's book did not adhere to the commonly accepted standards of editing and book design that we rely on for understanding what we read.

So where did these standards come from? Mostly from a printer named William Caxton.

WILLIAM CAXTON

William Caxton has a lot to do with your ability to read the words on this page. He brought the first printing press to England. He printed the first books in English, and many of the design norms we expect to find in our books were developed by him and other printers of his time.

Caxton (c. 1415–1422 to 1492) was born in the county of

Kent not too far from London. He was apprenticed at about the age of 14 to a wealthy textile trader named Robert Lange. Caxton became a successful merchant, and in 1453, he settled in Bruges, Belgium, to ply his trade. On one of his business trips, he stopped in Cologne, Germany, where he saw his first printing press.

Impressed with the invention's business potential, Caxton decided to learn the new craft of printing for himself. At the same time, he worked on translating a well-known courtly romance from French into English. Published in 1475, Caxton's *Recuyell of the Historyes of Troye* became the first work—fiction or non-fiction—printed in the English language.

It was also a bestseller—seriously—and this was the point that convinced Caxton to switch from buying and selling cloth to manufacturing and selling books. So in 1476, he arrived in Westminster, England, with that country's first printing press. He went on to translate several more books, one of them the first non-fiction book printed in the English language, a how-to on playing chess. He also printed the works of Geoffrey Chaucer and Malory's tale of King Arthur, *Le Mort d'Arthur*.

What does this early printer have to do with spelling and the English language?

Everything, as it turns out.

HOW DO YOU SPELL APPLE?

If you're in a conversation and say the word "apple," it doesn't matter how you spell the word. You could spell it appel, appyl, appelle or appill while your listener could spell it upil, awppell or opell. As long as a transfer of information is oral, spelling counts for nothing.

But as soon as you put a word on paper, its writer and its reader must agree on how it is spelled so that it can be understood. Not only that, writers and readers need to agree on the use of punctuation, and of conventions such as paragraph indents. Even among those who love to text, tweet, or chat online, conversational norms abound so that folks can understand one another in print. In fact, these online forms of communication are analogous to riffs in jazz. A musician needs to understand chords before changing the way they are used just as those who use Twitter need to understand the basic rules of English before bending them.

If you have any doubts about this, if you think this grammar stuff is just so many silly rules, try this experiment. Below are two examples of a short excerpt from *David Copperfield* by Charles Dickens, originally published in book form in 1850. The first example appears as Dickens wrote it. The second example is the same passage without commonly accepted standards of spelling and punctuation. Note how the few changes made in these three sentences affect your reading speed and comprehension. Then multiply that impact by the length of a novel, and you might be ready to admit that spelling and punctuation matter.

FROM *DAVID COPPERFIELD* BY CHARLES DICKENS

The thought passed through my mind that in the face of my companion, as he looked upon her without speech or motion, I might have read his niece's history, if I had known nothing of it. I never saw, in any painting or reality, horror and compassion so impressively blended. He shook as if he would have fallen, and his hand—I touched it with my own, for his appearance alarmed me—was deadly chill.

THE SAME PASSAGE, WITH A FEW CHANGES

The thot—passt through my mind—that in the face of My Companion, as He looked upon Her, without speech or motion I might have read his nieces history, If I had known nothing of it. I never saw in any painting—or reality horror and compassion—so impressively blended. He shook (as if he would have fallen) and his hand (I touched it with my own) for his appearance allarmed mee, was deadly chill.

When Caxton arrived in Westminster with his printing press, he faced a muddle of English spellings and usages. So in addition to becoming his country's first commercial printer, Caxton also became its first editor. Along with other early printers such as Richard Pynson, Caxton set language and type design conventions that we use to this day.

But why go to all that trouble?

IT'S GOOD FOR BUSINESS

Caxton could have copied the spelling and punctuation of whatever writers brought into his print shop. It certainly would have been easier. So why did he choose to set standards for the books he printed? Why did subsequent printers choose to follow the standards he and a handful of other early printers set? The answer lies in the story I just told you about my friend Carol. Readers want and need their reading material to adhere to accepted standards of spelling, punctuation, design, and clarity so they can concentrate on what its author is communicating. They buy books that do this. They don't buy books that don't.

Having standards is also good from a bookseller's point of view. Can you imagine the chaos involved if booksellers, even the digital kind, had to stock books in London English and Boston English and Sydney English and Toronto English? Can you imagine how hard it would be if you wanted to read the latest novel by your favorite author but it wasn't available in your particular brand of English?

SELF-PUBLISHING AND THE LOSS OF STANDARDS

You've probably tripped across your fair share of misspellings in books. But the fact that they stand out indicates that misspellings are uncommon. For centuries, booksellers and readers had the luxury of judging books by their content without worrying about their spelling or grammar. So it came as something of a shock in the late 1990s when the market was flooded by the first wave of volumes put out by companies that call themselves "self-publishers."

Why? Because self-publishing companies do not require authors to purchase editorial services, so authors often skip this part of the process to save money. As a result, many self-published books are full of misspellings, sloppy writing and grammatical errors.

In addition, the interior design services sold by self-publishing companies do not equal the quality we've come to expect in our books. (See Chapter Seven, page 63, for more details about interior design and quality standards.)

When books with these low quality standards were placed on the shelf next to high-quality books, booksellers quickly discovered that readers chose the high-quality books. It didn't take long for most bookstores to refuse to stock self-published books and for libraries to refuse to buy them.

The failure to maintain editorial and design standards is the main reason self-publishing has such a bad reputation. And because self-publishing companies use digital print technology—they market it as print on demand or P.O.D.—that form of printing earned a sour reputation as well. To this day, many bricks-and-mortar stores as well as libraries avoid books published by well-known self-publishing companies.

Independent publishers, on the other hand, understand that quality matters. A good independent publisher knows the same thing that William Caxton did: You can sell more copies of a high-quality book.

LEVELS OF EDITING

Traditionally, there are three levels of editing a book: Developmental, copyediting and proofreading.

• Developmental editing: This takes place before a manuscript is considered finished. Developmental editing is akin to sculpting clay with an author's words substituted for the clay.

In fiction, a developmental editor is concerned about developing character, honing plotlines or clarifying parts of an author's work. If we're talking about non-fiction, a developmental editor is concerned about the depth of an author's research or the overall organization of a book.

Nowadays, it is very rare for a traditional publisher to invest the time and money in developmentally editing a book because of the cost.

• Copyediting (also called line editing or, sometimes, simply editing): This is the form of editing that most people associate with correcting text. But good copyediting is more than just catching a misspelled word or a missing comma.

Copy editors fact-check books where possible to make sure that recipes are accurate, that the years of someone's birth and death are correct, that a cited title is right, that Abraham Lincoln's first vice president was indeed Hannibal Hamlin.

Copy editors also check for consistency within a book. If a character has a scar over his left eye on page 27, is it still over his left eye when it's mentioned again on page 171? Are place names spelled the same throughout a book? Most readers assume that writers keep all of these details in their heads but considering how long it takes to write a book—anywhere from a few months to a few years—details can and do get lost down the memory hole.

• Proofreading: This type of editing happens after the interior design of a book has been applied to its text. At this stage, often called first pages (see definition in the Glossary at the end of this book), a proofreader's job is to check the work of the typesetter as well as to conduct a final check for spelling and punctuation errors.

EDITING = BEING STRIPPED NAKED

I can usually tell how often a writer's been published by the vehemence he or she puts into the words "I don't need to be edited." To new writers, the thought of anyone finding something to correct or change among their carefully selected words or (horror of horrors) uttering a word of criticism about their work feels a lot like being stripped naked in public.

One of the best ways to get over this fear is to do some editing yourself. Here are two examples of actual cover letters sent to a traditional publisher. Before you read them, put on your editor's hat and pretend it's your job to decide whether your publishing company would agree to take on these works. How long does it take you to make that decision?

(Author's note: A few personal details in these letters have been changed but their tone and quality has not been touched. And honest, I didn't make them up.)

EXAMPLE ONE

Another Query letter from a silly boy who likes to take pictures and make up elaborate stories. The book I am proposing is a trilogy, with a continuous story line but the order and format of the stories are not important, each can stand on there own. It takes place in a mythical land where the quick and the dead can exchange gifts. It attempts to marriage good and evil and shows the consequences of this struggle over power. It is full of visual imagery that twist and turns constantly. I am interested in a story with written text and visual imagery layered together and multiplying the meanings in a variety of ways letting the reader compound the meanings according to the readers own experience. I would like to keep each book from 20 to 30 pages.

EXAMPLE TWO

I have completed two of the many Samuel Gambone mysteries; the third and fourth are in progress. But I wonder why I bother.

Can I get a publisher to at least read them, either one? No! I have written to 14 publishers and the answers are usually the same. 'It doesn't fit our lists.' Or, in three cases, 'We usually deal with agents; please look at the writers' guide for a listing of agents.'

So I send a dozen letters to agents. One was too busy, another said our philosophies do not agree, most said no, but three said send the manuscript and money ($250.00 in one case) and they would read and critique the manuscript. And those three said that this critique did not mean that they would represent me or my books.

Is the entire publishing industry, and the agenting business filled with people like this? I read the *Writer's Market* and selected only publishers and agents who claim to handle murder mysteries. My books are that: there is murder, there is suspense, there is mystery, there is crime. Maybe my books are too complex for the small minds of this industry to comprehend.

Maybe the books are just no good; that my writings are infantile or incoherent. (My lover of forty one years used to accuse me of that but I have gotten even.)

If this attempt meets with the same failures as my previous efforts, I shall quit writing and open a house of ill-repute. Many men think that that is the only thing women are good for. They may be right. At least, that business would supplement my small income.

Thank you for your consideration.

OK, how long did it take you to decide whether your

publishing company would take on either of these books? Not long, I'd bet. But did you once consider either of these writers on a personal level before you made that decision? My guess is that you based your decision purely on their words, not their personal characters.

My point is this—editors care about the impact of words on a page. If someone points out a better way to write something or corrects your grammar, please do not take it as a personal attack. One of the primary jobs of a good editor is to make sure writers do not make fools of themselves in public.

There are a couple of other considerations to take into account before we leave the topic of editing. Nowadays, many traditional publishers comb the ranks of self- and independently-published books looking for titles to add to their offerings. When they do this, they consider the subject matter of a work, the author's marketing efforts, and the quality of the finished product. If having your book picked up by a traditional publisher is a possibility you like to entertain, you enhance your chances of success with good editing.

When looking for an editor, choose one with book editing experience. I realize your high school English teacher was a stickler for spelling and grammar but that does not translate into good book editing.

One more consideration—editing is akin to a dance between an author and an editor. I have heard horror stories about professional authors with great writing credentials being reduced to near tears by editors who confuse critiquing with disparagement. No one has the right to trash your hard work or denigrate your efforts. With this in mind, I recommend that when shopping for an editor, you ask for references from other writers and check them.

There are a great number of terrific editors out there who can and will work with you to make your work sparkle. Don't settle for anything less.

CHAPTER SIX

Book Covers

I HAVE NO IDEA who first said you shouldn't judge a book by its cover but it's a lot of hooey. We all judge books by their covers. In fact, publishers have developed something of a code to help us find what we like to read by just looking at a cover.

For example, a purple cover with a man and woman in the obvious mood for something intimate screams romance. Covers featuring castles often denote fantasy novels. A quiet country cottage splashed with a dash of red is a cozy mystery novel, while a cover that proclaims an author's name in far bigger type than the title screams "bestselling author."

This chapter is not about how to use your desktop publishing software to create a great cover. There are lots of good books written specifically for that purpose, and there are too many variations on that theme to cover here.

Nope, this chapter is about recognizing what sort of cover works for your type of book, how to instruct a designer to create what you want in the most efficient way possible, and some of the technical stuff you should know if you want to use one of your own images on the front of your book.

Let's begin with two simple cover design exercises.

COVER DESIGN EXERCISE ONE

Empty one of your bookshelves. Pile the books up on a table or the floor or your bed, wherever it's convenient.

Now go through the pile(s) one book at a time. Take a short glance at the cover—no more than three seconds—then put it in one of two piles, the "I like this cover" pile or the "I don't like this cover very much" pile. Don't think about this at all. Make snap judgements.

Once you've gone through all of the books, take the "I don't like this cover very much" pile and spread the books out so you can see them all simultaneously. (This works best if you spread them out on the floor.)

Walk around your pile slowly, taking note of the similarities among the covers. View the books upside down to see if there are similarities that catch your eye. Is there a color in common among them? Are they all text with no images? Is the size of the type too small to read comfortably? What is it that you don't like?

Now do the same with the covers you do like, asking the same questions. Make a list of your likes and dislikes, then put your books back where they belong.

Repeat this process during a visit to a bookstore by paying close attention to what attracts your attention and what does not. Do this again at your public library and at the drugstore where they have all those romances and thrillers for sale.

There's no right or wrong here, just gaining an awareness of what attracts you and what doesn't.

COVER DESIGN EXERCISE TWO

This exercise involves spending some time on Amazon.com. Begin by thinking about where you would find your book in a library. In other words, what categor(ies) does your work fall under? Use these terms to do a search on Amazon. Study the covers of the books that are like yours. What do they have in common? Are there certain images or styles that appear frequently? For example, you can differentiate a romance novel from a cookbook at a glance by the covers because each of these segments of the book market always display distinctive features.

What about the books in your segment of the book market? What features do they have in common? How do these features apply to your book? Take some time to imagine this. Make sketches. Look for images in magazine or books or among your own photos that you believe reflect what's in your book.

DESIGNER INSTRUCTIONS

These exercises may seem like a lark but they have a very important purpose. I've designed book covers for many years and know several designers involved in the same work. To a person, we all agree that clients who have a clear idea of what they're seeking expend less money getting what they want. The worst clients are those who cannot articulate their vision but expect a designer to create exactly what they see in their mind's eye. "I'll know it when I see it" is a prescription for frustration and disappointment on both sides.

I'm not advocating dictating a cover (red goes here, blue goes there, etc.) because at its best, this type of design is a collaborative process. What I am advising is that you think through how you want your readers to perceive your book when they see its cover. Work to articulate this before seeking a designer to carry out your vision. You will save everyone a lot of hair tearing as well as time and money.

TEXT VS. IMAGE

Of all the ways you can treat a front cover, all text is the least expensive. You don't need to worry about getting the technology just right for an image. You don't need to worry about copyright. You just need to choose the right font.

On the next page, you'll find two examples of the same cover using text only. Which one would you buy, based solely on its cover?

I sincerely hope you picked the cover on the next page. Why is this cover a stronger candidate for sales?

First, the title emphasizes the book's most important selling point—making money. In the cover below, the words "Six Figure Income" don't stand out from the rest of the title.

Second, two of the four dollar signs on the second cover are off the page. This oddity attracts our visual attention for a fraction of a second longer than in the cover below. More attention = greater sales potential.

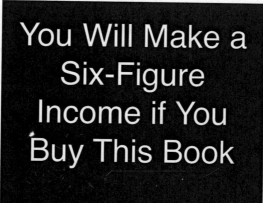

Third, the author's name is de-emphasized in the cover above. As a general rule, this is a good practice unless you are widely considered an expert in the field covered by your book. In fact, unless you're a four-star celebrity, it generally makes no sense at all to put your picture on your book. People have a wide variety of reactions to human faces, both positive and negative. If a potential reader doesn't like your haircut or your designer eyeglasses or the poodle you're holding in your arms, you've probably lost a sale.

If these two covers were ice cream, the first one would be melted vanilla. The second gets into rocky road territory.

Take my advice—if you're going to use just text on your

front cover, go for the rocky road. And the best way to get rocky road is to hire a good designer. (For tips on finding a designer, please see pages 35 and 70.)

USING IMAGES ON YOUR COVER

Most book covers benefit from the addition of a good image on the front—and sometimes the back—cover. If you put 20 designers in the same room to ask what constitutes a "good" image, you'll probably get 20 differing opinions. But there are some qualities and specifications they do agree on.

1. An image enhances but does not overwhelm a book's theme.

How many of you have read a book with a cover that didn't match its contents? Puzzling, isn't it? Or seen a book with a front cover so compelling, you don't remember its title? You can't do a search on Amazon with the key words "woman in bright yellow bikini bottom." But if you remembered the title of the book was *Blazing Beach Babies Take Vegas*, you'd find it immediately. In other words, it's important to balance the impact of the image with the impact of the title.

2. Unless there's a compelling design reason to do otherwise, use images that are clear.

This may seem self-evident but photographs that appear in focus on the small screen of a digital camera can turn out to be fuzzy, hazy and/or blurred when they appear full sized. Do check.

3. If you want to use someone else's artwork on your cover, be absolutely sure you have permission to do so—in writing. And don't assume that ancient artwork in a museum is not protected by copyright. If the museum owns it, the imagery belongs to the museum. And they can be pretty touchy about misuse of their imagery.

4. Unless you pay the price for a high-resolution file (300 DPI TIFF, see the next section), images taken from the web will not print clearly. And they may belong to someone else which

means you have a copyright problem if you use it without permission. I know there are a number of folks who want to believe that if something appears on the web, it's in the public domain. Don't you believe it.

HOW TO USE YOUR OWN IMAGES ON YOUR COVER

If you do not have the equipment and software needed to correctly format your own digital images, the best alternative is to locate a local copy shop or graphic designer who will do this work for you. (See pages 35 and 70 for tips on finding a good designer.)

If you want to format and manipulate your own images for print, there are some technical specifications you need to know. If you decide to use a self-publishing company for your book and want to use your own cover image, their technical requirements are the same as those described below.

THE PRELIMINARY TECHNICAL STUFF

A publishing colleague once commented she heard white noise every time I started to explain the technical stuff connected with images or printing. I know this tech stuff is not everyone's cup of tea but I've seen the disappointment on people's faces when I have to tell them that a treasured image won't work on the cover of their book because of technical problems that can't be fixed or overcome. So being conversant with the basics is a good idea.

Here are a few general rules about images that even the most non-geek person can start with.

- The images you view on a computer screen or digital camera are made by pixels of light.

- Images on paper are made up of dots of ink.

- You need far more dots of ink to make a great image than you do pixels of light.

- You can reduce the size of an image and it will still look great. If you have a digital photo that measures 18 x 22 inches, you can reduce this to 4 x 3 inches and the image remains clear.

- You cannot enlarge an image. It will blur or look as though it was constructed of blocks. If you have a digital image measuring 5 x 7 inches and you enlarge it to 6 x 8 inches, it will look fuzzy and out of focus.

- Most digital cameras take images in a format known as JPEG (short for Joint Photograhic Experts Group, the people who created this format). This format is perfect for viewing on a computer screen. It is not the best choice for printing on paper, however. Here's why.
A JPEG (also JPG) is a compressed file format. When you open and make changes to a JPEG file—such as cropping or altering color—you change the information in the file. When you save it, the computer squeezes (compresses) this information. When you reopen (expand) the same file, the computer must interpolate (make educated guesses) about the data to make an image appear on your screen. During this process, some of the old data as well as some of the new is lost. Over time and use, this open-change-save process degrades the quality of the image. With a JPEG file, it's always best to open the original file once, make a copy then make your changes to the copy.

- The best format for printing on paper is called a TIFF (Tagged Image File Format). A TIFF contains more color information by far than a JPEG which means that a TIFF puts more ink on the paper. You can, with certain stipulations, convert a large JPEG file into a TIFF.

GETTING A BIT MORE TECHNICAL: THOSE DOTS

If you used a magnifying glass to look at a black and white photograph in a newspaper, you would see that it is made up of dots. The more dots gathered together in the same place, the more black that place appears. The fewer dots, the more gray it appears. No dots equals white.

Our eyes are incredibly good when it comes to blending those dots together so that we see pictures of high school students competing in sports, the latest car from Detroit or politicians with their mouths open.

The same blending phenomenon occurs when we look at a computer screen. Every image you view on a screen— whether it's a digital camera or a Kindle or your iPhone— consists of pixels of light in various colors. (For purposes of this discussion, let's stipulate that a pixel is similar to a dot.) If the number of pixels is right, we see images of turtles or airplanes or the gowns worn by actresses on their way to the Oscar celebration. If the number of pixels is not correct—if there are too few of them—we'll see colors but no images.

We express the number of pixels we need in order to make an image appear on a screen as "pixels per inch" or, more commonly, PPI. Just about every image you view on a digital screen is 72 pixels per inch. In fact, if you're on a website where the images load slowly, chances are they are more than 72 PPI.

The JPEG format is ideally suited to the web because it needs less information (pixels) to create an image. In fact, the JPEG format was created for this purpose.

The same paradigm is true for photographs in books. These are made of dots of ink as in a newspaper, not light. The trick is, our eyes need more dots of ink to perceive an image than they need dots of light. We measure these dots in "dots per inch" or, more commonly, DPI.

The TIFF format we discussed earlier is ideally suited for print because it is designed to hold lots of information (dots).

If this is confusing, think about this in terms of paint.

Let's say you have a wall that's eight feet high by ten feet wide, and you've been asked to paint it yellow. If all you have is a cup of paint in your gallon bucket, you might get some paint on every spot of the wall but it would be mighty thin. That's equivalent to a JPEG. If you have a full gallon of paint, however, you'd definitely be able to cover that wall and it will look yellow. That's equivalent to a TIFF.

OH, ONE MORE THING: RGB VS. CMYK

OK, OK, I know this tech stuff is getting to be a bit much, but if you want to do this yourself, I can't leave out this key piece of information.

When we look at a color image on a digital device, what we view is actually made up of bits of three hues: Red, Green and Blue (RGB). This color system is the only one used in images created by a light source such as those in computers and digital cameras.

When this same image is printed on a paper, the colors are made up of four elements: Cyan, Magenta, Yellow and blacK (CMYK). If your book on paper will be printed from a PDF file, all of your color images must be in CMYK or they will not print. Period. Nope, not at all.

This simple conversion can be done in an image manipulation program such as Photoshop Elements.

SO WHAT, EXACTLY, DO YOU NEED FOR YOUR BOOK?

The short answer to this question is: A 300 DPI TIFF in CMYK that's the same size or slightly larger than the size that will appear in your book.

If that's clear to you, great. If not, read on, and I'll explain how to do this yourself.

CONVERTING PRINT IMAGES TO DIGITAL

Let's say you plan to publish a family history, and you have a picture of your great-grandfather that you want to use on your cover. There are two ways you can do that: Scan your photograph or take a picture of your picture.

SCANNING

Nowadays, you can purchase a computer printer that also functions as a scanner, a copying machine, and a FAX. Scanning uses exactly the same technology as a digital camera except that the object being scanned lies flat on a glass surface while it is photographed.

If you own a scanner, you need to investigate the software that applies to it in order to know how to create what you need. I own a Hewlett-Packard Officejet that prints, scans, copies, and FAXes. (Now, if I could get it to vacuum the office, it would be perfect. But I digress.)

When I use the scanner, I select the resolution (Dots Per Inch or Pixels Per Inch) for the scanner to use when it copies my image. I also pre-select (before I scan) what format I want the scanner to create (JPEG or TIFF).

Most scanning software merely runs the scanner. It does not allow you to manipulate images once they are created. In order to do that, I recommend using Adobe Photoshop Elements. This is the smaller version of the big kajuna in image manipulation, Adobe Photoshop. Elements costs far less than the full Photoshop (under $100) and will do everything you need to create images in the right size and format for printing on paper.

While you have the digital image open in Elements on your computer, be sure to reduce its dimensions (width x height) to a size that's close to what you need for your book.

Remember, you can reduce the dimensions of an image and it will retain its clarity. You cannot enlarge an image. It will become distorted.

Also change the color system from RGB to CMYK.

TAKE A PICTURE OF THE PICTURE

If you own a digital camera, you can use it to take a picture of your printed image. Experiment with the lighting— natural light or incandescent (not fluorescent) lighting is the best choice—to get a crisp, clean photograph.

Depending on your camera and the software that comes with it, you may be able to convert your photograph into a 300 DPI TIFF. If your camera's software does not allow this process, use Adobe Photoshop Elements to get this done.

Be sure to reduce your image's dimensions (width x height) to a size that's close to what you need for your book, and change the color system from RGB to CMYK.

CONVERT YOUR DIGITAL IMAGES TO PRINT-READY IMAGES

Just about every digital camera out there takes pictures in the JPEG format. Does that mean you can't use them for the cover of your book? Not at all. Here's how you convert your JPEG photographs to print-ready TIFFs.

1. JPEGs from digital cameras are usually large in size— 18 x 22 inches is not uncommon. (To ascertain the size of the JPEGs in your camera, consult your owner's manual.)

2. In order to create a usable TIFF, you need to do two things—reduce the dimensions of the image and increase its resolution (DPI).

3. Download the images from your camera using the software supplied by its manufacturer. Every camera's software is different and you may be able to perform steps 4–6 using that software. If not, I recommend using Photoshop Elements to do these steps.

4. Make a copy of your original image.

5. In Elements or your camera's software, open up the menu that gives you an image's size. In Elements, you will find an option called Image Size under the Image menu.

6. Increase the Resolution of your image to 300 pixels per inch.

7. Decrease the width and height of your image to what you need in your book. Remember, you can decrease the width and height of an image without distorting it. In Photoshop

Elements, you can change either the height or the width and the other will change in proportion if the boxes at the bottom of this menu are checked. When you finish this step, the total Pixel Dimensions should not be higher than where you began.

8. Be sure to change your image to CMYK.

9. Do a Save As and choose to save your file in the TIFF format. Consult the Help menu in your particular software for specifics on how to do this.

Your digital file is now print ready.

THE BACK AND SPINE OF YOUR COVER

Next to your front cover, your book's back and spine are its most important real estate—in terms of marketing. And I'm not just talking about the back cover copy.

On the next page, there is an example of a full cover set up to be printed. Let's take a tour of a book cover, shall we?

THE SPINE

The next time you visit your local bookstore, station yourself approximately ten feet away from its shelves, and spend some time gazing at the books lined up on them. As I'm sure you're aware, most books are presented to their potential readers by their spines.

As you look at the spines in front of you, pay attention to those that jump out and those that are difficult to read. This is an important consideration when designing a book cover. Spines are so narrow, there's no room for fancy design work or anything illegible.

A book's spine is utilitarian to the nth degree, and it should be designed this way.

One other bit of information you should know—a full cover, as you see it presented on the following page, is never constructed until the final page count of a book is known. Why? Because the spine must be exactly the right size for the type of paper and number of pages to be bound within it.

Some printers supply book cover templates with the spines calculated to three decimal places. Other printers simply give you a formula that's used by a designer to create a book cover with the correct spine. If you hire a designer, tell them what you want to see on the spine and make sure they understand how a spine is calculated.

THE BACK COVER

These are the elements that are standard on a back cover: Subject line, retail price, back cover copy, bar code, and publisher's name. Details below.

SUBJECT LINE

The top line in the upper left corner of a back cover is the subject line. If a book is a novel, the subject line reads FICTION. If the book is about baseball, it would read SPORTS/BASEBALL.

The choice of a subject line is not casual. The Library of Congress dictates subject areas for books, as do book distributors. A correct subject line is an aid for booksellers and librarians when it comes to figuring out where a book should be shelved which, in turn, is an aid to sales.

RETAIL PRICE

If your book is published by a traditional publisher, its retail price will be set by the publisher. You won't have a say in that decision.

If you independently publish your book, you need to understand the math behind a book's retail price before you set it so you don't lose money. You can find out more about book math in Chapter Ten, page 99.

Self-publishing companies often set a book's retail price at a level that covers the cost of printing while it ensures a profit for the company. Depending on the company, an author may or may not have a say in this decision.

BACK COVER COPY

There are two opinions about what should appear in a book's back cover copy, and there's no right or wrong here. The only criteria is what you believe best enhances a book's sales potential.

Many people, and I count myself among them, prefer to read 200 words of description about what is in the book. But many publishers believe that a vivid quote from a well-known figure can sell more copies of a book.

Many publishers opt for a mix—description followed by one or two catchy quotes. This is actually a pretty good compromise IF the quotes capture the flavor of the book. In other words, simply putting the quote "Fabulous..." —*New York Times* is worthless.

If the thought of writing your own cover copy gives you a case of vapors (writers are notorious for their reluctance to sell themselves), here's an exercise to help you get over that.

1. Select a small number of books you've read and write copy for them. Two hundred words, no more.

2. Keep the sales jargon to a minimum (eliminating it all together is even better) and simply tell someone else what this book is about. When you're done, read what the publisher printed on the back.

3. Now do the same for your own book.

If this exercise doesn't take care of your nerves, ask another writer or your editor to pen your back cover copy.

PUBLISHER'S NAME

It is not absolutely essential for a publisher's name or logo to appear on the back cover. But it's not a bad idea. It's another sign of credibility. If there is no publisher, a sharp-eyed reader may think it's an amateur project and put the book back on the shelf.

BAR CODE

If you want to sell your book commercially, it absolutely must have a bar code on the back cover. A bar code is actually your book's ISBN (International Standard Book Number) refashioned so it can be read by a scanner. Many bar codes also include a book's retail price.

If you're publishing with a traditional publisher or a self-publishing company, they supply the appropriate bar code with the correct ISBN and price. If you publish independently, your printer may supply the bar code for your back cover. If not, you can purchase bar codes from the same place that sold you your ISBN.

CHAPTER SEVEN

Interior Design

I ONCE WAS given a book by a publisher's rep because I admired its cover. The cover was dramatic, a down-deep close-up of part of a dark red flower against a stark black background. Being a gardener, I was sure the subject matter would interest me—how plants have been used as medicines through history.

But as much as the outside of the book attracted my positive attention, the inside annoyed me. At least half the pages had footnotes, and many of those footnotes took up most of the acreage on the page. In fact, some of the footnotes were longer than the pages they were meant to enlighten.

It was like trying to read two books simultaneously, and after slogging along for fifty pages or so, I gave it up as a bad job. The material was interesting but the way it was presented on the page interfered with my ability to read it.

Have you ever had such an experience, trying to use a book only to discover that the information on its pages is presented in a way that makes it unusable? Or have you been bogged down in the middle of a page that's been set all in *italics* because the frilliness gets in the way of the story?

What I've just described are problems of interior design. In this chapter, we will cover the basics of good interior design so that you can improve the way your text looks on the page, recognize good text design when you see it, and know how to figure out if a graphic designer is text savvy or not.

If you decide to typeset your interior yourself using a word processing program such as Microsoft Word, please turn to page 123 for advice on the proper way to do that.

THE TOP TEN RULES OF GOOD INTERIOR DESIGN

There are lots of guidelines for good text design, and some rules. The two most important rules, however, are these:

1. EVERYTHING THAT HAPPENS ON THE PAGES OF A BOOK SHOULD ENHANCE A READER'S EXPERIENCE.

2. IF A READER BECOMES AWARE OF A BOOK'S TEXT DESIGN, THE DESIGN IS NOT DOING ITS JOB.
Text design, when done well, should be invisible.

Why are these rules the most important? Because readers buy your book to learn something new or for entertainment or both. Any time something within the book breaks a reader's bond with its content, this spell is broken. The reader once again becomes aware of laundry to be folded, dishes to be washed, or a bathroom to be cleaned.

Books are portals into another world or a different way of thinking or a new skill to be learned. Clumsy design is akin to setting up an obstacle course for your readers to negotiate, and few readers appreciate that sort of interference.

3. LESS IS MORE WHEN IT COMES TO TYPE STYLES.
Type styles such as *italics* or **bold** or SMALL CAPS, are the textual equivalent of a pointing finger.

Italics

Of course there are good reasons to use type styles but they are generally limited to specific cases. For example, the title of a book, if it appears within a paragraph, is always set in italic type. That's part of the code we expect to find in our books, that titles are italicized.

There's an additional reason not to use too much italic typeface—legibility. Our eyes read, in part, by recognizing the shapes of individual words, not letters. And this is best done with Roman typefaces, not italics.

I have seen novels that tell two concurrent stories, and sometimes one of the stories appears all in italics. This does separate one story from another but it is lazy design. There are far better—more legible—ways to achieve this same effect. If you decide to hire a designer for the interior of your book, ask him or her how they would handle this dual-story situation. If they tell you that one of the stories could be all in italic type, look for another designer.

Bold

Boldface type is often used in headers such as the one you see above this paragraph.

Like *italic* **typefaces,** too **much bold** is **too much** of a good thing. **By trying to draw attention** to many points in a text **with bold or** *italic* **typefaces, you end up with** paragraphs **that are** tiresome **to read.**

SMALL CAPS

SMALL CAPS or ALL CAPS are another way to show emphasis, to draw attention to a particular phrase. They are best used, like boldface, in headers.

SMALL CAPS AND ALL CAPS ARE ESPECIALLY DIFFICULT TO READ OVER LONG STRETCHES OF TEXT BECAUSE EVERY LETTER IS THE SAME HEIGHT AND WIDTH. OUR EYES ARE DESIGNED TO SCAN LANDSCAPES WITH SMALL, MEDIUM AND LARGE ELEMENTS IN THEM AT THE SAME TIME. CAN YOU IMAGINE TRYING TO READ A WHOLE BOOK IN THIS TYPE STYLE?

4. SAVE QUOTATION MARKS FOR DIALOGUE.

Many authors, particularly "academic" authors of non-fiction, have a pronounced predilection for placing "quotation marks" around words that have a "specific meaning" within their field. We're not talking about "quotation marks" used to "signal dialogue" but to draw attention to "certain" words or phrases because they are unfamiliar or used in a way that's "outside their norms."

The "overuse" of "quotation marks" leads to "paragraphs" that look like "forests of punctuation." The "best way" to handle this within the design of a book is to use "quotation marks" or *italics* the first time a "new term" or "word" is introduced. Make sure this "original appearance" is accompanied by a good definition then eliminate the "quotation marks" or *italics* on subsequent appearances.

5. DON'T USE UNNECESSARY CAPITALIZATION.

Like All of The type style Usages listed above, the Overuse of Initial Capital Letters draws too much unnecessary attention to Itself. This is One Time that Adherence to the Common Rules of Grammar is a Really Good Idea. The Best Reference for the rules of capitalization is the *Chicago Manual of Style*.

There are exceptions to any rule when they are done to enhance content. For example, A. A. Milne uses initial caps in his *Winnie the Pooh* books to add to his gentle humor.

But Generally speaking, when it Comes to Capitalization, Use only What is Necessary.

6. CHOOSE YOUR FONTS FOR THEIR LEGIBILITY.

A font, just to be clear, is a specifically designed set of letters, numerals, and punctuation marks. For example, the font used in the text throughout this book is Century Schoolbook. It is an example of a serif font.

This font is called Helvetica. It is the default font used by many computers. It is also commonly used in road signs because in large sizes and short phrases, it is eminently legible. This is an example of a sans serif font.

This font, Handwriting-Dakota, is considered a specialty font. Think of fonts of this type as icing on a cake. They are meant to be pretty but reading a whole book in a font like this would be maddening.

So what's the difference and where do you use which type of font? Let's take a close look at the same letter in a serif and then a sans serif font.

This is a capital S in the font called Century Schoolbook. Notice how the width of the letter varies from thin to thick and back again. While this is not necessarily a part of every serif font, it's pretty common among them.

The part of the letter that's circled is the serif. These extra flairs on the terminal parts of a letter actually aid our reading when the size of the letters is small, as on the pages of a book. Visually, serifs hold words together, aiding our ability to recognize them by their shape.

This is the capital S in a sans serif font called Helvetica. Notice how the width of the letter is the same throughout. While this is not characteristic of every sans serif font, it's pretty common.

The absence of serifs (terminal flairs) on this type of font makes them a good choice for short pieces of text such as headers or signs on interstate highways. But they're not the best choice for big blocks of text in the size you commonly find in a book because when letters lack serifs, it is more difficult for us to discern the shapes of words.

7. USE APPROPRIATE FONTS.

One of my favorite writing teachers told me this story. She was leading a class in short story writing. After working for a few weeks, her students handed in their work for her editorial critique.

One of the stories she received was typed all in a *Gothic* font. Now my friend exhibited a lot more patience than I would under the circumstances. Reading a whole story in this font would be a tough slog. But she persevered.

When she returned the stories to her students, they started getting them ready for submission to magazines for publication. Without mentioning names, the teacher talked about font selection and legibility. But when the time came to mail out submissions, that same student had the same story still in a *Gothic* font.

Why? my friend asked.

Because my story takes place during the Middle Ages so the font is appropriate for the story, the student said.

No. No, no, no. Remember the most important rule of all—text design is always done with the needs of the reader foremost in mind. Given the chance to purchase a Medieval novel set in something like Century Schoolbook or the Gothic font called *Lucida Blackletter*, no reader chooses *Lucida Blackletter*.

Choose your fonts for their legibility first. Save the *Lucida Blackletters* of the font world for decorative purposes only.

8. KEEP THE NUMBER OF FONTS YOU USE TO A MINIMUM.

I think **that** simply trying to read YOUR way **from the beginning to the end of this paragraph** *will make the* **reason for this rule** readily apparent. Using too many fonts *is a common mistake* among those who are just learning to design with text.

If you use too many fonts, your text starts to look like a ransom note from a movie with the letters cut out of a magazine. Like hot sauce, a bit of font diversity goes a long way.

9. JUSTIFY YOUR TEXT.

Most of the text in this book is justified. This means both edges of a block of text are aligned vertically, the common way to set text in a book.

This paragraph is left justified. This means the left edge is always in a straight line and the right edge is ragged so that it zigs and zags visually.

This paragraph is right justified. The right edge of the text
is in a straight line while the left is ragged.

This paragraph is centered. The center of
each line of text lies beneath the center
of the lines above and below it.

There are good reasons to alter the justification of some of the text in a book.

Headers can be centered.

If the width of a column
of text is narrow, it's best
to use left justification.

When you quote, you often right justify,
—the attribution

But most of the time, text blocks in a book on paper are justified on both sides. The appearance of justified text is neater, and visually, it's better at holding sentences and paragraphs together.

Yep, legibility again.

10. ADHERE TO THE ESTABLISHED RULES OF INTERIOR DESIGN FOR YOUR TYPE OF BOOK.

Even if we don't think about it much, we expect to find certain types of text design in certain types of books. For example:

this\\'th̲i̲s̲\adv (15c) is the way we expect to find entries in a dictionary or thesaurus.

A. The steps in how-to books are often numbered or lettered so that the numerals are set out ahead from a block of text.

Novels, short stories and essays are the easiest books to design because the text is in an uninterrupted flow such as you find in this sentence, and in most of the sentences you will read in this book.

Spend some time looking at the insides of books like yours. Remember that good text design enhances the material in a book so that it is useful for the reader. Generally, keeping your text design as clean and simple as possible is the best way to go.

If you hire a graphic designer to do the interior of your book, be sure she or he has book design experience. In every discipline and craft, there are permutations among its practitioners, and graphic design is no different. A great web designer may be clueless about how to design and set type for a book on paper. Someone who's an ace with advertising or logo design may not know how to design for legibility.

Ask to see samples of a designer's work. And bring samples of book designs that you like so that the expectations are clear on both sides.

HOW TO FIND A GOOD TEXT DESIGNER

There are any number of book designers to be found online. But I would seek a more local option through the recommendations of local businesses that use brochures, through local college administration offices, from mid-sized or small publishers or university presses, from non-profit organizations (especially those that use newsletters) or arts organizations. Remember, when you publish independently, you are more than a writer, you are a business person. Be careful who you hire, and check references.

CHAPTER ONE
First Page of a New Chapter

Think of the first page of a new chapter (such as the example above) as the opening credits of a movie. If you wish to use decorative elements, this is the place to strut your stuff. For example, I used the same character (from a font called Kooksters available on the website www.dafont.com) to open my chapters as I used on the front cover. This gives my book design continuity throughout.

In contemporary works of fiction, chapters are usually numbered but have no titles, though there are wonderful exceptions to this. (See the works of Alexander McCall Smith for example.)

Books of essays, short stories, and poetry most often use the beginning of each new entry as a chapter opening.

Works of non-fiction, generally speaking, use both numbers and titles in their chapter openers.

Page numbers generally appear in the upper or lower outside corners of a page (see example on the page to the left). Sometimes they are centered on the bottom of the page. Do not put page number on the inside corners of a page where readers cannot see them as they flip through a book.

In fiction, page headers, such as the one seen at the top of the page to the left, are normally the title of the book on one side with the author name on the other.

In books of essays and short stories, headers generally reflect the title of the pertinent story or essay on one side with the title of the book or the author's name on the other.

In non-fiction, page headers are used to help readers find particular content. For example, in this book, the title repeats on the left-hand page while the chapter name appears on the right. This was done to aid readers who may be seeking one particular section or topic.

It has long been the custom in book publishing to begin a new chapter only on a right-hand page, such as the one you see to the right. But this more formal way of setting up a book is not as *de rigueur* as it used to be. Adhering to this guideline can mean a blank left-hand page.

PART ORGANIZATION

Generally speaking, the parts of a book follow this order:

Half title page (no subtitle or author name)

Full title page

Copyright page (Please see page 183 for a full description of what belongs on your copyright page.)

Table of Contents

Introduction

Acknowledgements

Dedication

Text of the book

Epilogue

Glossary

Endnotes

Index

For more information on the parts of a book and their organization, I recommend the *Chicago Manual of Style* which describes the standards throughout the industry.

CHAPTER EIGHT

Printing and Distribution

WHEN IT COMES to printing, you have two technologies to choose from—offset and digital (often called print-on-demand). As with so much in the world of book publishing, there are advantages and disadvantages to each choice.

When the digital printing of books first became viable and commercially available in the early 1990s, it was easy to tell the difference between a digitally-printed book and one that was done via offset. Digital type on the page was not sharp and crisp. Pages within a digitally-printed book were often not bound properly so the type from one page to the next was not aligned. The paper quality was noticeably poor and covers were noticeably flimsy.

The first bindings for digital books were pieces of special adhesive tape on the spine, and printing on them was not possible. In the words of a publishing colleague of mine, digital books at that time bore no resemblance to "real" books.

A lot has changed since then. Now it's all but impossible to tell the difference between offset and digitally printed books. So why choose one process over the other? That is actually more of a an economic question than a printing question.

Here are some points to consider as you choose a printing method.

THE ADVANTAGES OF DIGITAL PRINTING

• The machines that print books digitally use much the same technology as the printer you use with your computer. Like your personal printer, digital book printing gives you the flexibility to print as few or as many copies of a book as you wish.

In addition to printing services, some of the larger digital print companies include distribution services. Let me give you an example of how this works.

I use a company called Lightning Source (www.LightningSource.com) to print my books. Lightning Source is part of the Ingram Content Group, the largest book distributor in North America. If you ordered your copy of this book from Amazon, your order traveled from your computer to Amazon, from Amazon to Lightning Source where a single copy of this book was printed, placed in packaging bearing Amazon's return address, and shipped to you.

An order for one copy = one copy printed and sent to its buyer.

If you wanted to order 20 copies of this book from Amazon.com for your writing group (and you would do that, wouldn't you?), your twenty-copy order follows the same path.

• With digital printing, the cost of printed books is paid as books are ordered. The only upfront costs of digital printing are those associated with uploading digital files and the production of proof copies.

• As long as the digital file for your book exists, you never run out of copies of your book.

• You do not need to warehouse copies of your book.

• There is no wasted paper, no copies to throw away, and far fewer returns than with offset printing. It's a better deal for the use of natural resources.

THE DISADVANTAGES OF DIGITAL PRINTING

· The cost-per-page for printing digitally is greater than for offset. This difference grows less all the time but at this moment, digital printing is still more expensive than offset on a per-copy basis. (For a fuller discussion of the money side of book publishing, please turn to Chapter Ten, page 99.) Like offset, the cost of digital printing varies from printer to printer, so shop around for the best price and service package.

· You cannot print hardcover books with dust jackets digitally. You can print hardcover books but the covers are printed in a style known as paper-on-boards. You commonly see this type of cover on full-color how-to books.

· Unless you make special arrangements, you cannot print spiral-bound books digitally.

· One last caveat: Digital printing machines and the inks they use are designed to work with specific types and sizes of paper. This means your choice of paper is limited.

THE ADVANTAGES OF OFFSET PRINTING

· The per-copy cost of books printed by offset is less than digital.

· You can print hardcover books with dust jackets or with spiral bindings.

· You can choose among a wide array of different papers for the interior pages of your book. This is particularly important if you are publishing a high-end coffee table or art book.

THE DISADVANTAGES OF OFFSET PRINTING

· It is economically unfeasible to print less than 500 copies of a book via offset. In fact, it's really not a great idea to print less that 1,000 in order to get a good per-copy price.

· All of the printing costs are paid when the printing is

completed but before the books are shipped. In digital printing, you pay for books as they are printed.

• Because you have to print so many at the same time, books printed by offset must be stored in facilities with air quality control (for dust) and temperature control (so moisture cannot degrade the books). This means that in addition to printing costs, there are costs for warehousing, packing, and shipping.

• If books don't sell, they must be disposed of, adding to the waste stream.

• Once all the books in an offset print run are gone, the book is gone unless you place another order for 1,000 copies. At that point, before you invest, you have to ask yourself if you can sell an additional 1,000 copies. This is the reason why, in commercial publishing, few hardcover books ever get a second print run. The number of copies in an initial print run is calculated to cover a publisher's costs if they all sell. Most publishers understand that once this is accomplished, the chances of selling a thousand more books is slim.

DISTRIBUTION IN GENERAL

Distribution is the process by which books are delivered to readers. For example, bookstores order copies of the books they wish to have in their stores from distributors such as Ingram and Baker & Taylor. Specialty stores often buy copies of books from wholesalers who supply other products in addition to books.

There are a number of ways for an independent publisher to handle book distribution. The first, and easiest, is to use a printer that has distribution services or maintains a network of responsible distributors with whom they work.

Distribution can be a thorny issue, one that needs to be clearly addressed before you spend money publishing your book. If you have your heart set on publishing through traditional channels, be certain that the company that agrees to publish your work can distribute it where your target readers can find it. This may seem like an obvious part of the traditional publishing process but it's not necessarily so, especially when it comes to very small publishers.

If you are investigating self-publishing companies, it's important for you to understand where your book will be sold. Most self-publishing companies maintain an online store, and that may satisfy your needs. But if you want your books available on Amazon or for order by bookstores and libraries, you need to choose a company that can make that happen for you, or enable you to do it on your own. In other words, the cost of purchasing copies of your book is reasonable enough to allow you to resell them at a profit.

In independent publishing, distribution is key. All of the printers I've listed at the end of this chapter provide different forms of distribution. I would suggest you begin your search there so you understand the many options open to you.

DISTRIBUTION THROUGH AMAZON.COM

Amazon.com was the company responsible for upsetting the traditional publisher/bookseller sales relationship that existed for centuries. Without the sales outlet provided by Amazon (and other online booksellers), independent book publishing would be nothing more than printing.

Even if you print your books on your own desktop printer or at your local copy shop, you can make them available for sale on Amazon as long as they have an ISBN. Here's a list of the most important sales options at Amazon.com.

PUBLISH THROUGH CREATESPACE

Amazon maintains its own books-on-paper publishing company with CreateSpace. Every book published through CreateSpace is available for sale on Amazon.

Createspace does supply author services such as editing and some design or you can create your own PDF of your book to upload through your CreateSpace account. There's more about CreateSpace at the end of this chapter.

PUBLISH THROUGH KINDLE BOOKS

Kindle is one of the easiest-to-use electronic publishing outlets currently available to authors. The Kindle Store is, of course, accessed through the Amazon.com website. For more information about this form of publishing, please see Chapter Seventeen, page 157, on electronic publishing.

AMAZON ADVANTAGE

For a small annual fee, you can maintain an Amazon Advantage account. This membership gives you access to the Amazon warehouse where your books are stored until they are ordered. Amazon lets you know when supplies get low, and you send more to the address they give you.

Advantage members are responsible for shipping their products to Amazon. Also be aware that books sold through Amazon Advantage are subject to the standard trade discount of 55 percent for Amazon, 45 percent for the seller. See Chapter Ten, page 99, for a full explanation of the term Standard Trade Discount.

AMAZON MERCHANT

Amazon maintains a vast online marketplace for all sorts of products, including books. Their Merchant program works this way: You pay Amazon for the privilege of listing your products with them. When orders for your products arrive at Amazon, these orders are sent to you for fulfillment. In other words, you function as your warehouse.

There are some printers, BookMasters among them, that will act as your warehouse and fulfill orders received through an Amazon Merchant account.

Merchant account fees vary according to the sales plan you choose, and are available on the Amazon.com website.

PRINTERS

The following is a very short list of printers to get you started. My personal recommendation for the first-time independent publisher is to choose a company that will print your book digitally one copy at a time, and distribute it for you. This is an excellent way to get your toe in the water, and learn the business without a major investment. After you've gained some experience, you can always switch to another way of printing and distributing your work. Or you may find you made the choice that suits you best the first time.

LIGHTNING SOURCE (LSI)
www.LightningSource.com

Part of the Ingram Content Group. Books printed digitally by LSI are distributed by Ingram. They are also available on Amazon and other online booksellers. Independent authors who set themselves up with an account with Lightning Source can order as many copies of their book as they wish at any time.

Lightning Source is not an author services company. They do not provide editorial or design services. They are a printing company with distribution facilities through Ingram and the partnerships Ingram has established with international distributors.

Ingram also distributes books electronically. They also provide scanning services for authors who wish to bring their out-of-print books back into print.

Lightning Source does provide ISBN bar codes. You give them your ISBN and they provide the bar code. Independent publishers who use this company are responsible for purchasing their own ISBNs.

Printing costs vary depending on the dimensions of a book, whether its interior is in color or black & white, and how many books are printed at one time. Many self-publishing companies as well as traditional publishers such as MacMillan now use Lightning Source for digital book printing.

LSI also provides offset printing services through a variety of printing partners. Books printed via offset are not eligible for distribution through Ingram.

CREATESPACE

www.CreateSpace.com

Part of Amazon.com. Books distributed by CreateSpace are available only on Amazon. Authors can order as many copies of their books as they wish at any time. Independent publishers who use CreateSpace also gain easy access to distributing their books electronically through Amazon's Kindle store. At this point in time, Amazon provides a Kindle app (a free bit of software) that enables readers to download books from the Kindle store to a wide variety of non-Kindle readers such as the iPad, iPhone, Android, and Blackberry.

Of all the ways you can publish electronically, no one seems to have made it easier than CreateSpace. They have a service that converts books from Microsoft Word or PDFs into Kindle-ready books.

CreateSpace does not print books via offset. It does provide fee-for-service editing, cover design, and interior design. Be sure to use an ISBN that you purchased so there is no question who is the publisher of record.

BOOKMASTERS GROUP

www.Bookmasters.com

Bookmasters is a full-service printing and distribution company. It prints books digitally and by offset, and will handle the conversion of your book into a digital format. They also have warehouse services, and will handle the billing and shipping details of distribution.

THOMSON-SHORE, INC.

www.ThomsonShore.com

This employee-owned company has been in the book printing business since 1972, and has long had a good reputation among graphic designers and publishers for quality offset work in hardcover and softcover books. T-S also prints books digitally but not one at a time. You have to purchase a certain quantity and pay for them all at once. They have also expanded into the author services arena.

CHAPTER NINE

Marketing: Guidance and Some Advice

IT WOULD BE easy to devote this entire book to the subject of marketing. In fact, there are a lot of books out there on this subject, some of them good, some not so much.

The following list includes four marketing books culled from the dozens I've read. In my opinion, it's wise to include both face-to-face and internet strategies in your marketing campaign. These four books cover the main strategies to consider when it comes to marketing your book.

PUBLICIZE YOUR BOOK
by Jacqueline Deval

Jacqueline is very experienced in the book marketing field, and this gives her advice the down-to-earthiness that I truly appreciate in a book like this. This is hands-on marketing with lots of examples.

THE ZEN OF SOCIAL MEDIA MARKETING
by Shama Kabani

I know, I know, it's difficult enough to keep up with your email and everything else competing for your attention but you may be just the type of author who's a natural at social media. There are lots of good ideas in this book as well as a sensible perspective on what can and cannot be done via social networks. Even if you never decide to become part of the Facebook community, there are lots of other social media paths to explore, and this book is a good one to have in hand while you do that.

SELL YOUR BOOK ON AMAZON
by Brent Sampson

Brent seems to have made a career out of studying the paths and byways of Amazon.com and explaining how they work. Amazon is too important a sales outlet to ignore, and while I wouldn't recommend putting all of your marketing eggs in this basket, it has become the go-to site for anyone interested in any book. Even if readers decide to purchase your book elsewhere, chances are good they'll look you up on Amazon first so you'd be wise to cover the basics, and this book's a good place to start.

PLUG YOUR BOOK: ONLINE BOOK MARKETING FOR AUTHORS
by Steve Weber

Every time I give a workshop on book publishing, someone in the class raises a shy hand to ask about marketing. "Am I really going to have to get out there and talk to people in person?" is more or less how the question is framed.

Now I can talk to a room full of people with a minimal amount of nervousness but lots of folks pale at the very idea. Thankfully, there are now tons of opportunities to plug your work online, and Steve supplies down-to-earth and pragmatic strategies to marketing you can do in your pajamas.

CRAFTING AN APPROACH TO MARKETING YOUR BOOK

I've been involved with marketing for many years. As a newspaper reporter with a weekly column devoted to arts and entertainment, I was on the receiving end of tons of publicity materials, all of which gave me a lifelong appreciation for what works and what doesn't.

Later, as the marketing manager for a book publisher, I moved over to the sending side of the publicity equation. These experiences taught me a lot but the most important lesson, I think, was that it is impossible to ever be done with marketing. No matter how many efforts you make, there will always be something more you should have done, could have done, would have done if you'd just had the time. Don't fret over this assessment, just recognize that it's part and parcel of every marketing effort.

The second and equally important lesson is that no one markets a book as well as its author. No one. In other words, there is no substitute for your personal attention and energy.

The opposite side to both of these coins is that it is very easy to feel so overwhelmed by the wide variety of marketing ideas that you can't get started. In the following pages, I'm going to recommend a way to select ideas from the marketing books in the preceeding list (or your own personal favorites), and then provide you with a basic plan that gives you a good platform to structure your personalized marketing efforts.

Ready? Of course you are.

CULL THE BEST IDEAS

Begin by reading all of your marketing books—either the ones I've recommended or your own favorites—straight through. Don't stop to do anything or do research, just read.

Every time you find an idea that sparks your interest, jot

it down on an index card or a separate slip of paper, including the page number and book title so you'll know where to find it again, and then move on.

Keep on plugging until you reach the bottom of your reading pile, and have a sizeable stack of index cards. Now take a deep breath, go through your cards slowly, and consider all of the ideas you've jotted down with these questions in mind:

- Will you actually follow through on this idea?

- Can you imagine yourself taking the actions needed to accomplish this idea?

- Do you have the expertise to accomplish this task or do you know where to acquire that expertise?

Make two piles of cards as you go through this process— the ideas you will work on and the ones you won't, at least not now. Keep your won't-do-now pile handy. These ideas probably just need more time to flower.

THE BOX-O-STUFF APPROACH TO MARKETING

Even though I can't see your pile of "will-do" ideas, I'd be willing to bet they have some sort of common denominator. We all have comfort zones, and we work to keep the planned events of our lives in those comfort zones. The key here is to recognize this, and use it as the starting point for structuring your personal marketing campaign.

As you look at your cards—and the time and effort they represent—you may have no idea where to start. Here's a story to help you get over that feeling.

The main character of this tale is named Bob. Bob was the sales manager at the publishing house where I was the marketing manager so now you know this is a true story.

Like many industries, publishing has an ebb and flow. Late August and December are traditionally dead times while you can't seem to run fast enough in April and October. We were in one of those can't-run-fast-enough times at our office. Bob and I had mounds of paper on our desks, each piece screaming for our undivided attention. The phones were ringing, people were asking questions. It was crazy.

Bob finally threw up his hands, and went down to our book warehouse to get a midsize box. When he came back, he swept every piece of paper off his desk—never looked at any of them—and put the whole lot in his "box-o-stuff." Then he calmly took the piece of paper on the top of the pile, did the task dictated by it then reached for the next piece of paper.

Ten minutes later, I was in the warehouse looking for a box. And you know what, taking all of those to-dos one at a time made us both more efficient. As an extra-added bonus, we got to throw out many of the items that sifted down to the bottom of the box because their urgency had expired.

To this day, whenever those frenetic, overwhelmed feelings creep into my life and my desk is a mass of inscrutable piles of stuff, I go find a box. If the idea of marketing freaks you out, get a box, throw all your marketing ideas into it then pick the one that ends up on the top, and work on it. There is no real right way or wrong way to begin marketing, no matter what the experts tell you.

Unless it's not beginning at all.

EVERY DAY

There are lots of things you do every day—brush your teeth, eat breakfast, clean your contact lenses. My most strenuous marketing recommendation is to add one more regular item to your daily routine. Do one marketing action every day. Send out a targeted review copy. Follow up on an email or telephone call. Contact a local venue, library, PTA, or club to ask about scheduling an event with you and your book.

Believe me, most authors do nothing or very little in the way of marketing no matter how much people like me try to encourage them. If you do one thing a day, you will be far, far ahead of everyone else. It will be your book capturing all the interest in your niche, not your competition.

One other added attraction for a daily marketing effort is this: You won't get bored, you won't get stale, you'll see your efforts afresh instead of dreading an eight-hour grind.

I live in snow country, and shoveling teaches you this same lesson: You clear a path one shovelful at a time.

KEEP TRACK OF YOUR EFFORTS

As you work through your marketing ideas, make notes about everything you do, including your investment in time. I am very low-tech when it comes to this part of the marketing process. I use one of those composition books that are part of every back-to-school sale for organizational tasks like this. If I think of something and scratch a note on a piece of scrap paper, I make sure it gets taped it into the notebook. If someone gives me a business card, it goes in the notebook. I write down every phone number, every idea, every name, every lead. The notebook goes with me in the car, sits next to my computer on my desk, and attends every meeting I attend because you never know when inspiration will strike or someone shares the best marketing idea you've ever heard.

When your first marketing efforts are well underway, take the time to sit with your notebook (or whatever your choice of organizational method happens to be) to assess your efforts. What worked? Where were the dead ends? Have you left any unturned stones that should be turned?

Think about the individual tasks that make up your marketing efforts in terms of your time investment, and your return on that investment. Some tasks, such as writing a great press release, take a lot of time but once you're done, that press release becomes a regular part of your marketing outreach. That's a good time investment.

But what about the time it took to set up a signing at your local bookseller only to have two people show up? Not a great investment. (This, by the way, is the most common scenario for a signing by anyone other than Stephen King or J.K. Rowling.) Cross that off your list of efforts for the future.

After a careful assessment, go through your plan and your stack of will-do ideas, select another one, then start the process all over again.

In my experience, marketing gets easier the more you do it, just like anything else. In time, you may find it possible to move outside your comfort zone. Or you may not. The point is the doing. Every day, remember.

THAT MARKETING FRAME OF MIND

Marketing is all about letting potential readers know about your work. If you don't tell them, how will they know about it?

Whenever I hear an author making scared noises about marketing, the words I hear most often are "But I can't sell myself." The phrase implies the idea of cold calling, of knocking on a stranger's door to get them to buy your book.

But that is not marketing. That is sales, and the difference is key. When you market, you talk about your work just like a software engineer, an arborist, a town clerk, or a bicycle touring guide.

"What do you do?"

"I write."

"Oh really. What do you write?"

If you've taken the time to set up your marketing program properly, your reply to a question like this should include the gift of a postcard or bookmark or business card with a picture of the cover of your book, information about how it can be purchased, and at the very least, your authorial email address so your conversational partner can get in touch.

Marketing is an email to your friends and colleagues and family that says: "Hey, guess what? My book is on Amazon!"

Marketing is adding a line to your email signature that goes something like: "Mary Rose Webster, author of *Get a College Education for Free* now available on Amazon.com."

Doing anything less is false modesty. And admit it, aren't you proud of the fact that you have published your book? Of course you are. Books are HUGE projects, and getting to the finish line gives you the right to talk about your work.

A BASIC MARKETING PLAN

Putting the claims of marketing miracles to one side, at its most basic, good marketing is focused attention combined with good research skills and outreach efforts. Which is a fancy way of saying you need to figure out who your likely readers are, where you need to go to attract their attention, and how to get there.

A full marketing effort need not put pressure on your wallet. In fact, the most important elements in any successful book marketing effort are email, postcards, copies of your book, a press release, and digital copies of your cover that can be successfully used on the web and in print.

In order to help you get started, I've included a basic how-to-do-research for your book below. That's followed by a short list of outreach suggestions.

MARKET RESEARCH ONLINE

No matter what you do to market your book, the single most important piece of information you need to know is who your potential readers are. This is your target market, and when you identify it, all of your other marketing decisions will be tailored to serving it.

Ideally, a writer should take some time to identify her or his target market before setting pen to paper but usually we don't. So now your book is written and ready to publish. How do you identify your readers? You begin with some extensive online research.

COMPARATIVE TITLE ANALYSIS

When traditional publishers consider a book for publication, they want to know two things: How your book is different from other books in the same category, and how it is like other books in the same category. If you're publishing your book independently, you want to answer the same questions. These may sound like opposing thoughts but they are the basis of potential reader identification.

For example, if your book concerns the history of the American Civil War, it's probably not going to be of interest to someone who reads mystery novels and collects cookbooks. But it would potentially be of interest to Civil War re-enactors, people who blog about American history, antique gun collectors, and visitors to Ford's Theater in Washington, D.C. Readers with these interests have probably read books about the American Civil War, and would read another if it had a different perspective on historical events or added previously unknown information to what they know.

Using this Civil War history as an example, let's stipulate that it is like other books in the same category but it's also different because it adds new information about the life of Robert E. Lee.

How would the author of this book begin to identify its potential readers? By doing a comparative title analysis. Before the internet, this type of research was painstaking at best. Now it can be done online, mostly on Amazon.com.

START YOUR RESEARCH

Of all the sales techniques on display at Amazon.com, probably the most powerful is the way the website customizes book suggestions for every individual visitor, especially for those consumers who make purchases from the site. For every title on Amazon, there is a list of books that other buyers purchased on the same topic. In other words, these suggestions represent a niche.

A niche is best defined as a sub-category in a larger section or genre of the book universe. Examples of a niche include:

- Turning wood on a lathe among books on wood-working.

- Cozy mysteries as a sub-category in the mystery genre.

- Gardening in New England as a niche among gardening books.

- Books on 19th-century economics among books on economics in general.

Why is identifying and understanding niches so important? Because this is the arena in which your book is going to compete for readers and potential buyers. To return to our American Civil War example, the author of this title would benefit from knowing where readers with an interest in Robert E. Lee get their information about new books. Yes, it is also important to know where readers of Civil War books learn about new titles but by targeting this book's niche, the author's sales potential is increased.

There's another good reason to thoroughly understand your book's niche on Amazon. Since niches are smaller sales arenas, the sale of even a few copies can make a tremendous difference in where a title appears in Amazon's listings. Sales of fifty or a hundred units can make a book jump several spots in these niche categories. So the next time a reader with an interest in Robert E. Lee searches for books on this topic, this author's book could potentially be at the top of the list. And being at the top of the list draws more attention and, potentially, more sales.

FINDING YOUR NICHE ON AMAZON

How do you find your Amazon niche? Start by typing in the keywords of your book's subject area—American civil war, climate change, nature photography, historical fiction, how to make ice cream, whatever. Chances are good that the return on your search includes several dozen titles, at the very least.

Move through the pages that Amazon returns for your search terms, clicking on the titles that most closely resemble your book. When you reach an individual book's page, prepare to spend some time there. This is what you are looking for:

- The author's (or authors') name...
  so that you can look up his/her/their websites

- The price of the book...
  so that you know what the price range of yours should be.

- Who published the book...
  so that you can look on the publisher's website for information on other books in your niche.

- The other titles Amazon recommends so...
  you can do a search on them. These titles represent your companions in your niche.

- The member reviews because...
  members often recommend or mention other titles in the same niche. Follow up on these.

- Scroll to the bottom of the listing because...
  Amazon provides additional recommending services such as discussion groups in particular subject areas. Visit these to gather more information about your niche. Also look at the Listmania and "So You'd Like To" sections that appear at the bottom of many book listings. Again, follow the links there, gathering the same information as you go along.

Searching and selling on Amazon.com is worthy of a book all by itself. Lucky for us author Brent Sampson wrote one called *Sell Your Book on Amazon*. Please refer to that volume for more in-depth information.

NOW WHAT DO YOU DO?

Why should you care so much about discovering the outlines of your book's niche? Because each of the links provided by the books in your niche is a potential pathway to areas on the web in which you can find people with an interest in your subject area. Here are some suggestions on what to look for:

- Possible blurb writers in your subject area.

- Possible reviewers.

- Academic professionals who might consider using your book for teaching purposes.

- Organization websites with newsletters willing to mention your book.

- Bloggers who review books like yours.

- Websites that would consider publishing articles by you in the subject area of your book.

- Book discussion groups with an interest in your subject area.

- Author sites on places such as Facebook or YouTube.

Needless to say, keep track of where you visit so that when your marketing campaign is ready to roll, you can contact these places to share information about your book.

If you decide to pursue the traditional publishing path, agents and prospective publishers will expect to find a comparative title analysis in your book proposal. (See Chapter Sixteen for more on this topic.) And you should be aware that self-publishing companies often include something called a "comparative pricing analysis" in their package of services. What I just described in this section on Amazon is equivalent to an in-depth comparative pricing analysis.

BROADENING YOUR SEARCH: GOOGLE

Google's Book Search is an outstanding tool for both market research and also as a sales driver for your book.

Google has amassed a large repository of books in its database. This digital repository is searched through keywords. When you search for a keyword, your results pages display the titles of books and the exact pages where your search terms are found. Clicking on a book's link takes you to the page containing the keyword(s) you used as well as providing information about the book, and where it can be purchased. As a market research tool, Google Book Search is an excellent resource with results that can be cultivated in much the same way as those you find on Amazon.

BLOGS

Blogs are interactive websites where the blog host writes about a given topic. Readers can post their own comments on the host's musings, triggering discussions. In terms of market research, blogs are an excellent way to find who may be interested in your book's subject. As with everything else on the internet, blogs can be found by search engines such as Google.

The best way to approach blogs is to think of them as electronic word of mouth. Active blogs with large readerships have the potential to be great sales drivers with just one recommendation or a positive review of a book.

Plug Your Book: Online Book Marketing for Authors by Steve Weber provides more in-depth information about using the web to sell your book.

SOCIAL MEDIA

Social networking sites such as Facebook, LinkedIn and MySpace work on the principle of people finding each other and establishing contact, whether it is old friends from college or people with similar interests. These sites also maintain groups with members who share an interest in any number of topics, causes, organizations or the like. In other words, social networking sites are a collection of niches.

Like blogs, the group pages on social networking sites provide members an opportunity to comment about a group's topic as well as help gain insight into the scope of interest in a particular topic. To access these groups, you must become a member of the social networking site that hosts the group.

Social networks and how to market on them are worthy of a book all by themselves which is why I recommend *The Zen of Social Media Marketing* by Shama Kabani.

BASIC MARKETING MATERIALS

When it comes to preparing marketing materials, bear in mind this rule: The average consumer makes a decision about whether to buy or not buy in seven seconds. It may seem as though that rule wouldn't apply to the choosing of books but it does, far more than you think.

The people on the receiving end of marketing materials— whether it's for books or the latest car from General Motors— receive lots of this stuff. Tons, in fact, if you could weigh the digits in an email. So the marketing materials for your book need to get right to the point.

What constitutes a package of basic marketing materials? This list covers the basics.

1. Digital versions of your front cover in formats suitable for the web and print.

2. Digital and print versions of a one-page press release that includes a picture of your front cover, purchasing information for individuals and booksellers, and good contact information so a prospective reviewer or writer can get in touch with you. (You can download full-color samples of press releases from www.SonjaHakala.com any time.)

3. A full-color postcard with your book's front cover on one side. Your book's title, your name as its author, purchasing information (including the retail price), a short description, and good contact information are on the other side. Include a postcard in every book you send out. Keep them with you to use instead of business cards while you are marketing your book. Send them out as publication announcements to your family, friends, and colleagues. (You can view full-color samples of postcards at www.SonjaHakala.com)

In addition to the above, I highly recommend you create a website or host a blog dedicated to your book and about your work. If you'd rather not invest in a full-blown website, there are a number of free blogging services where you can get yourself set up in a relatively short period of time such as Blogger.com, Wordpress.org, and Typepad.com.

Make sure you include your web or blog address in absolutely everything you send out. Also be sure to take the time to set up an author's page on Amazon. When folks receive information about your book, chances are they will jump online to find out more about your and your work. Make sure they find something.

EIGHT MARKETING IDEAS TO GET YOU STARTED

A publishing colleague of mine, whom I consider something of a marketing whiz, once remarked that the best way to sell a book is to give away a book. No matter what else you do for marketing, nothing beats review copies.

How many? Fifty to one hundred is not out of line.

What do you do with them? Here's a list of eight suggestions for using your review copies.

1. Compile the following:

- A mailing list of print media outlets that will talk about or review your book.

- A list of blogs that review books.

- A list of blogs and print media that cover the same subject as your book.

Before you send out books, please do yourself the favor of contacting each of these outlets or people to ask for permission to send them materials. Not only does this show respect for prospective reviewers, it raises your profile just a bit because most authors do not do this. When they say yes, mail books, press releases, and other materials immediately.

2. Compile a list of story ideas to pitch to prospective media outlets that could feature your book. If your pitched story idea is accepted, be ready to fulfill any deadline requirements in a timely manner. Nothing makes an editor angrier than a missed deadline. By the way, the attention you receive from a well-placed article is more effective than a book review.

3. Keep a stash of eight books as a point-of-sale reserve with you at all times. Chance meetings and personal interactions have the potential to become a sales opportunity. If you don't have copies of your book, you will lose a sale and an opportunity to share information about your work.

4. Identify mavens. In his book *The Tipping Point*, author Malcolm Gladwell describes how three different types of people—connectors, mavens, and salesmen—with certain sets of social skills act as agents of change. Connectors are folks with the gift of bringing people together. Mavens are information accumulators, people who pay attention to markets and ideas in order to share that information. Salesmen are charismatic negotiators. In this part of your marketing adventure, you want to identify ten mavens in your life, and give each of them a copy of your book.

In this context, let's define mavens this way. They are people with an inherent interest in you, in books of your type or in books (like yours) that contain information of interest to them. In addition to their interest, these particular folks like to share their information with others both orally and in writing.

For example, if your book is about chess, get your book into the hands of someone you know who likes to talk about chess as well as play it. If your book is about wine, give it to an enthusiast who blogs about wine.

You want to let your mavens know that you've selected them because you understand their passion for your subject. In addition to a signed and personalized copy of your book, give them a copy of your press release.

Then ask them if, after they've read your book, they will review it on Amazon.com and other online venues such as Shelfari.com, LibraryThing.com, BarnesandNoble.com, etc. The goal is to have information about your book on every website where people talk about books or, if your book is non-fiction, about the subject of your book.

5. Contact your local newspaper. By virtue of living in the same area as your local newspaper's readership, you are a story ("Local Author Makes Good"). If your local newspaper dedicates space to the same topic as your work, send two copies of your book, one to a reporter who writes about your topic and one to the subject's editor. Staff names are often available on a newspaper's website but if you are in doubt, give the paper a call and ask for contact information to reach the right people.

6. Contact regional or state magazines or online newsletters. Before you send a book and materials to these outlets, take some time to study copies of the magazine in question. What sorts of stories do they normally cover? How do you as an author or your book's subject matter fit into their perspective? Look at the publication's ads. Whom do they target? Is this the same audience that you are trying to reach? Use this information to work up a short list of story suggestions to include in your personal letter—which accompanies a copy of your book—to the appropriate editor at the magazine.

Regional publications include business papers, arts and entertainment publications, neighborhood newsletters, church bulletins, and club or organization newsletters. These will probably function more as publication announcements but you would be surprised how much attention they draw.

7. Contact your college's alumni magazine. Most colleges print news for their alumni and will include, at the very least, a notice about an alum's achievements, such a publishing a book. Many will do longer stories.

8. Identify organizations with an interest that coincides with your book's subject area. Contact them to see if they use newsletters to stay in touch with their membership. Ask if they could use an article from you about their subject area. Send your contact one of your books. Ask about symposiums or conferences or other events where you could speak or sell your books.

Remember, the more you practice marketing, the easier it becomes. Just about every author I've known has trepidations and fears surrounding this subject. But I am sure that among the suggestions I've outlined here, and those you will find in the many excellent books on book marketing, you can craft a marketing campaign that fits your style.

The only sure thing you can say about marketing is that if you don't do any at all, no one will know about your book. And what's the point of that?

CHAPTER TEN

Get Out Your Calculator: This Is the Very Important Chapter on Publishing Math

CIRCULATE AMONG THE GUESTS at any writers conclave and you're sure to hear some variation on the following :

> "The only books publishers are interested in any more are blockbusters."

> "All publishers care about is the bottom line."

> "There used to be publishers who cared about literature, and would take a chance on a book."

> "They never marketed my book!"

All true statements, every single one of them. Of all the arguments that members of the writing tribe have with members of the publishing tribe, the most acrimonious are about money and marketing.

Here's a statement about publishing that you should hear but never do:

> "You don't get to publish book B if you don't sell enough of book A."

In traditional publishing, writers should root for the success of every book put out by their publisher because the money earned from those books pays for the production costs of the books that follow.

Think about this set of numbers for a moment:

- Out of every ten titles published in the U.S. by a traditional company, six will lose money, two will break even, one will earn a little money, and if the publisher is very fortunate, one book will make a lot of money.

But you know what's interesting about this scenario if you're talking about writers who independently publish their own work? Many of those "losers" become "winners."

This isn't magic. It's all about who gets to keep most of the money from book sales, pure and simple.

In order to make sense out of this discussion of publishing math, I need to take the time to explain three concepts: Setup costs, print runs, and something called the standard trade discount.

SETUP COSTS

Here's a bit of Let's Pretend to help you understand the important role that setup costs play in publishing. Let's say you've volunteered to make posters for a circus that's coming to town, and the only tools you have to make these posters are rubber stamps, one of every letter of the alphabet.

How long would it take you to get ready (set up) to make that first poster? You'd have to find the right-sized paper, locate ink pads, and experiment with the rubber stamps to get everything just right. That first poster would take you a bunch of time, wouldn't it?

But successive posters would take less time because you've been through the setup process already.

The concept is the same when you print on an offset press. Getting ready to print takes a lot of time. In offset printing, the setup costs can account for as much as half of the total cost of printing. As the printers say, "Once you've paid for the setup, it's only paper and ink." And in the relative scheme of things, paper and ink are not that expensive.

There are also setup costs in digital printing. It's part and parcel of making the pages of a book work for the reader, as we discussed in Chapter Seven, "Interior Design". The key difference is that once you've done the setup for a digital or electronic book, you don't have to decide how many copies to print because you can do it one at a time.

NOW WE GET TO TALK ABOUT PRINT RUNS

In the pre-digital print era of publishing, it was common for authors to ask one another "What was your print run?" In other words, how many copies of your book did your publisher print? In many respects, this print-run number told you how much hope a publisher had for a given book.

In traditional publishing on paper, a first novel from a new author gets a print run of 2,500 to 3,000 copies. For books in color such as art books or how-to craft books, the economics of printing by offset call for at least 5,000 copies. The print run for popular paperbacks (the least expensive book to print) can run much higher, into the tens of thousands.

Print runs are so much a part of the publishing ethos that it seems almost sacrilegious to point out that they really have nothing to do with the quality of a given book and everything to do with the printing technology used to produce it.

HERE'S AN IMPORTANT CONCEPT TO KEEP IN MIND

If Johannes Gutenberg had invented a way to efficiently and economically print one book at a time, traditional publishing as we know it today would have never existed.

That's right, the mechanics of book printing—setup costs and print runs—laid the basis for this industry a few centuries ago.

This is why the digital print revolution has wreaked such havoc on book publishing. If you take away the need to print and store thousands of copies at a time, you take away the core organizing principle of the book publishing industry.

THE NUMBER THAT WON'T GO AWAY:
THE STANDARD TRADE DISCOUNT

Way, way back when there were just printers and bookstores, distribution was a local phenomenon. Bookstores in London, let's say, bought copies of books they wanted to sell from printers in London with no one else in between.

When publishers evolved out of the printing industry, booksellers began to buy from them but still on a one-to-one basis. But as the number of publishers and booksellers increased, the logistics of this exchange got to be a nightmare for everyone involved.

There have always been aggregators in the book industry, people or companies who purchase copies of books for resale at a profit. The need for this function in this country reached a crescendo in the years following Word War II when U.S. government policy opened higher education to more people than before, more people began writing for publication, and the number of bookstores and readers grew. By the late 1950s, large distribution companies began to facilitate the movement of books from publishers to readers.

In addition to physically moving books from here to there, distributors keep track of three financial transactions:

- How many copies of which books are ordered by booksellers from publishers.

- How many unsold copies of which books are returned to publishers by bookstores for full credit. (This is commonly called returns.)

- How many copies of which books are paid for by booksellers.

Here's a simple overview of the distribution process:

- A bookseller orders a number of books by different publishers from a single distributor.

- The distributor aggregates orders from a number of

booksellers then places these larger orders with publishers.

• Publishers ship the ordered books to their distributor, at the publisher's expense.

• The distributor sorts all of the books it receives from the various publishers into individual orders for booksellers.

• Books sent to bookstores go onto the shelves. Books sent to online booksellers are often warehoused where they sit until ordered by customers. Some books sell. Some don't.

• At the approach of the 90th day of receipt of the books, sellers take those that aren't selling off their shelves or out of their warehouses to send back to their distributor for full credit. This is called returns. At the same time, they pay the distributor for the books they sold.

• The distributor figures out how many copies of which books were actually sold by booksellers, keeps its portion of those sale then pays the publisher its portion (45 percent of retail) of those same sales. The distributor is also responsible for sending returned books to the publisher for full credit.

When added together, these two portions—the one for the bookseller and the one for the distributor—constitute 55 percent of the retail price of a book. This is called the standard trade discount. This standard trade discount applies to all publishers whether they are independent or large traditional companies such as Random House.

SO WHAT IS THAT IN NUMBERS?
Let me show you the math involved with the standard trade discount using a $20 book as an example.

$20 (retail price paid by consumer)

$11 (portion of sale kept by the bookseller and distributor—the standard trade discount)

$9 (portion of sale paid to publisher)

By the way, you know those discounts that Amazon offers on nearly every one of the million titles it sells on its website? Those discounts for consumers are subtracted from the standard trade discount that Amazon receives. They do not impact the portion of sales paid to publishers.

STANDARD TRADE DISCOUNTS FOR eBOOKS

Electronic books and electronic bookselling are the brave new world in publishing today. As of this writing, the technical details as well as rights to publish, who's in charge of setting retail prices, and the rate of the standard trade discount are in flux.

Currently, ebooksellers are experimenting with trade discounts that fluctuate depending on an ebook's retail price. On Amazon, for example, publishers keep 70 percent of the sale of each ebook if its retail price is $9.99 or less. The percentage retained by a publisher falls to 45 percent if the publisher sets a book's retail price over $9.99. This has roused howls of complaint from traditional publishers who maintain it costs just as much to produce an ebook as it does to produce a book on paper.

By the way, there is evidence to suggest that the lower the retail price for an ebook, $2.99 or less, the greater the number of sales. Traditional publishers fight this concept, and many price their ebooks at the same or nearly the same level as a book on paper, a decision over which their authors have no control. Independent publishers, however, find they enhance their sales by pricing their work at the lower, impulse-buying level. Independent publishing author Joe Konrath has done some research on this subject and I recommend reading his blog to find out more: jakonrath.blogspot.com.

SO WHAT DOES A PUBLISHER PAY FOR, ANYWAY?

Since traditional publishing is, for the moment, the norm by which other types of publishing are measured, let's look at what they pay for, and how these calculations influence their decision on what gets published and what doesn't.

We need an example for our exercise. Let's make it a travel book by a first-time author named Ginny Webb, called *Local Fun: Good Times in Your Community*.

In order to begin our figuring process we need to know certain things about Ginny's book:

- How big is the advance for Ginny?

- How long it will take to edit her book?

- Does it needs images such as pictures or illustrations or maps?

- Does it require back matter such as a bibliography or an index?

- What is a good faith estimate on the costs of designing the cover and the interior.

- What are the projected marketing costs such as advertising and review copies?

- How many pages will it have and what are its dimensions?

- How many copies will be printed and what will they cost?

- What will it cost to warehouse this book?

On the next pages, you'll find a worksheet for *Local Fun: Good Times in Your Community* as it looks to a traditional publishing company. After that, we'll look at the projected costs if Ginny decides to independently publish her book.

ABC PUBLISHING WORKSHEET FOR:

LOCAL FUN: GOOD TIMES IN YOUR COMMUNITY

GINNY WEBB

- Author advance: $8,000*
- Editorial costs: $2,400
- Professional maps: $5,000
- Index: $450
- Interior and cover design/layout: $4,800
- Marketing costs: $2,500
- Number of pages in finished book: 256
- Dimensions: 6" x 9"
- Warehouse costs: $2,000

Total costs before printing: $25,150

*Author advances vary all over the map in traditional publishing. The size of an advance is largely determined by a publisher's perception of a book's sales potential, and its impact on a publisher's bottom line.

The size of a publishing house also figures into the size of an author's advance. Generally, small publishers (under 20 books per year) and university presses offer zero to $1,000 for an advance. Advances from midsized publishers (21 to 35 books per year) range from $2,000 to $3,500. Advances from large publishers (over 35 books per year) range from $5,000 up to to multiples of $1 million.

PRINT COSTS

For publishers, the most significant number on their worksheets is the per-copy cost of producing a book. So far, we know the total costs of *Local Fun* up to the point where it would be sent to a printer. Now we have to add the print costs into the total in order to calculate our per-copy cost.

Watch what happens to the cost per copy as the number of printed copies increases.

Total costs before printing: $25,150

Cost of printing 1,000 copies: $1,250

Total costs for book production: $26,400

Cost per copy: $26.40

Total costs before printing: $25,150

Cost of printing 5,000 copies: $4,600

Total costs for book production: $29,750

Cost per copy: $5.95

Total costs before printing: $25,150

Cost of printing 10,000 copies: $8,700

Total costs for book production: $33,850

Cost per copy: $3.38

Now that we have these figures in front of us, should we publish Ginny's book or not? Turn the page to find out.

MULTIPLY BY SIX

If you have a shelf of books nearby, grab one and locate its retail price. Now divide that number by six. You've just done a rough calculation to find the per-copy cost of the volume you have in your hand.

With few exceptions, publishers like to set retail prices that are six or (even better) seven times their per-copy cost. Of course, the other side of that calculation is what retail price the market will bear.

In general, the contemporary retail prices of travel guides run from $14.95 to $21.95. Using our divided-by-six formula, this means that the per-copy cost of a travel guide is somewhere between $2.49 and $3.66.

How does Ginny Webb's book stack up? Well, if we print 10,000 copies of it, the per-copy cost is only $3.38. When you multiply that number by six, you get $20.31 which makes a retail price of $19.95 feasible. (Keeping books under $20 is good business.) Eureka! She's in, right?

Hmmm, maybe.

ONE MORE QUESTION TO ANSWER

If you were sitting at a sales meeting in a largish publishing company, the calculations we've just done on these pages would be very familiar. In fact, if you decide to independently publish your own book, this is some of the work you should do. (More on that in a couple of pages.)

From all of the data we've gathered here, it appears that publishing Ginny's travel guide to local fun would be a good bet. But there's one more question you, as the potential publisher, need to ask: Can you reasonably expect to sell 10,000 copies of this book in a reasonable amount of time?

Travel books are consistent sellers, particularly in familiar brands such as *Lonely Planet* or *Rough Guide*. But travel information changes. Because of this, good travel guides should be updated every three years.

So let's refine our question a little bit: Can you reasonably expect to sell 10,000 copies of this travel guide in three years? What do you think? Which way would you decide?

IF YOU VOTE YES

If you decided to publish this book, Ginny Webb would be a happy woman. Bearing in mind that the average sale for any book published traditionally in the U.S. is less than 2,000 copies, you can appreciate the fact that *Local Fun* has a steep hill to climb in order to justify the publisher's risk.

Let's say the publishing house gets behind this book with some advertising money. At the same time, Ginny makes appearances as a speaker and guide in any venue that will host her. Review copies are sent to the media as well as to tourism websites and some well-known travel bloggers.

At first, sales are quite good. In general, the most favorable sales frame for traditionally published books is the first 90 days after publication. By the end of the first year, Ginny has sold 3,000 copies of *Local Fun*. By the end of the second year, the total is 4,500, and by the time it needs to be revised, she's sold 6,000 copies of her book.

Using the usual measuring stick employed in traditional publishing, Ginny Webb's book would be considered a failure. The publisher would opt not to bring out a revised edition. She would receive no royalty payments, and her book would be put out of print.

IF YOU VOTE NO

Ginny Webb, who's an entrepreneurial writer, would decide to independently publish *Local Fun*. She will sell 6,000 copies of her book, and she will be considered a success.

How? Let's repeat the worksheet from the previous pages to see how this book fares if it's published independently.

INDEPENDENT PUBLISHING WORKSHEET FOR:

LOCAL FUN: GOOD TIMES IN YOUR COMMUNITY

GINNY WEBB

• Author advance: $0

Even though it would be nice for someone else to pay her for the right to publish her book, Ginny believes her investment in her own work is worthwhile.

• Editorial costs: $800

We've covered the issue of editing in depth in Chapter Five, page 37, but it is fair to say that Ginny can do two things to save herself money in this area. First, she can carefully edit her work herself. Then she can seek the services of an editor with book experience. Chances are good she can get an excellent copyedit for $800 or less.

• Professional maps: $500

Of all the images that appear in books, maps are by far the most expensive to produce. They call for a focus on detail, knowledge of mapmaking software, and time. But there are a number of things that Ginny can do to keep the costs of her maps low. First, she can opt to purchase a single map of her coverage area to which she can (with permission) add numbers to point out the location of each of the areas of fun she covers in her book. Then she can hand-draw maps for each venue, checking their accuracy against online maps. (It's an infringement of copyright to simply use a map you find online.) Once her maps are complete, she can make digital copies of them either by scanning them herself (see the section on handling images starting on page 52) or paying to have them scanned to her specifications. Yes, it's more work this way but the hand-drawn quality, if well done, could add a nice local feel to her book.

Alternatively, Ginny could opt to put one map at the beginning of her book with the venues numbered, and provide detailed driving instructions in her text.

• Index: $0

If Ginny's book was an academic text, it would make sense to have it professionally indexed. But in this case, Ginny can create an index herself.

• Interior and cover design/layout: $2,000

Given that this is a travel book, the design of the interior is complex in comparison to the interior of a novel. Travelers rely on their guidebooks for ease of use so this is the most important place for Ginny to invest her money. Cover, interior design and layout are covered in-depth in Chapters Six and Seven.

• Marketing costs: $500

Ginny will need to print a number of copies at her expense for reviewers. It's also a good idea if she prints postcards with her book's cover on them and purchasing information about her book on the back.

• Number of pages in finished book: 256

- Dimensions: 6" x 9"

- Warehouse costs: $0

  Ginny is going to print her books digitally, one copy at a time, so she does not require a warehouse.

- Publishing costs such as ISBNs (Ginny buys a block of ten) and PCIP information (Publisher's Cataloging-in-Publication data—see page 186) and charges to upload her book to a digital printing house: $500

Ginny's investment: $4,300

PRINTING AND SHIPPING COSTS

As I noted in Chapter Eight on printing and distribution, the cost of printing a single copy of a particular book is dependent on a large number of factors such as: How the book is printed (digital or offset), its dimensions, the number of copies printed at one time, whether its interior is in color or black & white, how it's bound, the number of pages, whether it's a softcover or hardcover, etc.

That being said, I want to give you a real-world example of printing costs in this chapter so you can see how publishing math works. Because I use Lightning Source, Inc (LSI) for my printing and distribution, their printing costs are familiar so I am going to use them in this example.

If Ginny printed a single copy of *Local Fun* at LSI, that copy's printing cost would be $4.74. Shipping that single copy at the least expensive rate is nearly the same as the printing cost, $3.80.

So printing and shipping a single copy of *Local Fun* to her own home would cost Ginny $8.54.

Which is why I never recommend printing and shipping a single copy of a book if it can be avoided.

LSI, like most digital printers, offers a discount on the cost of printing in quantity. For 50 copies, the lowest number at which you receive a discount on printing, the per copy cost for printing falls to $4.50.

Now look what happens to the shipping cost. It will cost Ginny approximately $39 to ship 50 copies of her book to her house. That's $.78 per copy.

This means the total cost of printing and shipping 50 copies of *Local Fun* is $264 or $5.28 per copy.

But what about the copies that Ginny sells through Amazon and bookstores? How much do they cost? LSI charges a slightly lower price for copies printed to fulfill orders from booksellers, and this cost does not change no matter how many copies are ordered at one time. For *Local Fun*, the cost to Ginny per copy sold is $4.23.

These are the figures we will use in the next section.

HOW DOES GINNY EARN BACK HER INVESTMENT?

The moment Ginny finished writing her guide book, and decided to independently publish it, she became the chief financial investor in her work. And she has been a wise investor, determining what her book needs, figuring out what she can do herself, paying attention to quality, and choosing the right publishing partners to help her reach her goal.

Now that she has finished books in her hands, Ginny is removing her publisher's hat and replacing it with her sales hat. How many copies does she need to sell to earn back her investment? And what are her earnings if her sales match the traditional publishing scenario we just looked at? Take a look.

SALES THROUGH BOOKSELLERS

How much will Ginny earn each time she sells a book through an online or bricks-and-mortar bookseller?

Retail price of *Local Fun*:	$16.95
Minus the standard trade discount:	$ 9.32
Minus the printing cost:	$ 4.23
Ginny's profit per copy:	$ 3.40

In order for Ginny to recoup her investment of $4,300, she needs to sell 1,265 copies of her book through booksellers.

HAND SELLING

When an author sells a copy of her or his own book to a reader, this is referred to as "author sales," "back-of-the-room sales" or "hand-selling."

In Ginny's case, it is possible for her to lecture to local groups or lead kayaking or hiking excursions where her books are for sale. She can appear at writers' conferences to talk about writing her book. Whatever her outreach, these are the numbers for a single back-of-the-room sale. (Remember, Ginny's smart so she orders at least 50 copies of *Local Fun* at a time.)

Retail price of *Local Fun*:	$16.95
Minus printing and shipping cost:	$ 5.28
Ginny's profit per copy:	$11.67

Under these circumstances, Ginny needs to hand sell 369 copies of her book in order to recoup her $4,300 investment. Is that a reasonable goal for Ginny? Can she reach that goal? I figure it's a yes to both questions.

CONSIGNMENT SALES

Many stores, particularly if they are locally owned, dedicate shelf space to books by local authors. There's many an author who got his or her start by selling books from the trunk of a car.

On the other hand, authors who sell on consignment also tell stories about the horrors of bill collecting, of chasing retailers over small amounts of money. While there's no fool-proof way to avoid these bill-collecting woes, here are some methods to mitigate this hassle if you decide to sell books on consignment.

1. Create an invoicing system with two paper-

work trails, one for yourself and one for your sales outlet. Be methodical and meticulous about noting the number of copies you put on consignment, the date of the consignment, and the terms of the consignment. In general, consignments generate 40 percent of the retail price for the seller and 60 percent for the consignor (that's you). Payments should be made at 30-day intervals.

2. Visit the places where you consign books. If anything about the place makes you uncomfortable or raises your concern antennae, leave. Believe me, you won't be losing sales if you follow your instincts.

3. Check out the authors of other books you find on-site, search for them online, and if you find contact information, ask for recommendations about the consignee.

4. Ask about the seller's theft policy. If a book goes missing, how will that be handled?

5. If you do have to chase someone for money—or you never get paid—be sure to tell the consignee that you're going to spread the word about her/his business practices. Then do it.

THE CONSIGNMENT SALE MATH

Retail price of *Local Fun*:	$16.95
Minus the consignment discount:	$ 6.78
Minus printing and shipping cost:	$ 5.28
Ginny's profit per copy:	$ 4.89

One more item of considerable note on consignment sales: The price of gas and your delivery time must be a part of this calculation. There can be other benefits to consignment, particularly with local stores. They could become teaching venues or maybe they will host a reading for you. If you limit your consignments to a handful of reliable outlets, the support and encouragement you receive (and the local fame) can be a real boost.

In any case, if Ginny sold only by consignment, she would need to sell 880 copies. That is a very achievable goal.

Publishing math is one of the most convoluted parts of the business, and there are several permutations beyond those discussed here. The point here is to help you understand that there's more than one way to sell a book. All of them have their good points and their drawbacks.

TO SUM IT ALL UP

In our traditional publishing scenario, Ginny sold 6,000 copies of *Local Fun* but her efforts were considered a failure because her sales were not great enough to earn back her book's production costs. (Remember, production costs include an author's advance.) This is so common in traditional publishing that no one really talks about it—except authors.

When Ginny invested her time and money in her own book, she undercut traditional publishing's production costs by more than 80 percent. Some of these savings—such as the author's advance—are a natural consequence of independent publishing. But others, such as the cost of maps, were less because Ginny opted to do much of the work herself.

Nowadays, most writers who independently publish their work sell it through a combination of online sales (principally through Amazon.com), hand selling, and consignment. The percentages among these sales opportunities vary from author to author but let's finish off our *Local Fun* example by showing what a sample combination of sales could yield if we used the same sales figures as the traditional publisher who considered her book a failure when it sold only 6,000 copies.

Copies sold on Amazon.com:	2,000
Net earnings from Amazon sales:	$6,800
Copies hand sold by Ginny:	2,000
Net earnings from Ginny's sales:	$23,360
Copies sold by consignment:	2,000
Net earnings from consignment:	$9,780
Total number of copies sold:	6,000
Total net earnings:	$39,940
Ginny's initial investment:	$4,300

Some expenses are not accounted for in this scenario, the most obvious being Ginny's marketing time. But the point I want to make here is this: by independently publishing her own book, Ginny dramatically changed the odds of its success. Instead of failing to meet a sales threshold (10,000 copies) set by a publishing company, she has turned that "failure" into a success.

In addition to meeting her sales goals, Ginny reaps several additional benefits, such as:

• Recouping, in real terms, her investment.

• Making a profit on her investment.

• Creating an audience for subsequent books or revised versions of the same book.

• Proving she can market herself, a definite plus with traditional publishers if she decides to try that route.

• Enhanced self-confidence because she knows how to publish her own work, and sell it effectively.

- Credibility which can bring opportunities for speaking or teaching.

By the way, most published authors—whether traditionally published or independently published—find that the last item on this list is the greatest benefit of all.

SO WHAT ABOUT YOUR BOOK?

Now it's time to take a look at your own book from a publisher's perspective. What does it need to attract readers? Photographs? Drawings? An intricate interior design? An index or glossary or bibliography? Maps?

If your preferred publishing path is the traditional route, these are the kinds of questions a prospective agent or publisher will ask. These are all expenses, and add to the cost of a book project. The question in-house, if your book proposal makes it to that stage, is whether its sales potential is great enough to offset its production costs.

If you're interested in pursuing the path of independent publishing, the same questions apply. Maps, to use one example, are quite expensive to produce so if you're planning to publish a guidebook, you need to price this service as you create your budget.

If you plan to use a self-publishing company, you will be expected to supply your own images, illustrations, and maps to the specifications the company you choose sets out. And all of these add to the cost of design.

ONE FINAL THOUGHT

Most of an author's hesitation over whether to publish independently or not comes down to apprehension about the unfamiliar. That's normal, folks. We all hesitate on the brink of new ventures to ask "Can I do this?"

I would suggest that you change the question. Instead of "Can I do this?" ask yourself "How can I do this?"

If you get stuck or are not sure where to turn, drop me an email at Sonja@FullCirclePress.com. We'll talk.

CHAPTER ELEVEN

Publishing Path Two: Private Publishing

LET'S BEGIN WITH a list of the dominant characteristics of private publishing so we're all clear on how this is defined.

• A book that's privately published is not meant for sale to the general public.

• A book that's privately published has a limited audience.

• Generally, the author of a privately published book intends to give away all the copies that are produced.

• In many cases, the audience for a privately published book is personally known to its author. This audience is most often family members, friends, and colleagues.

Of all these characteristics, the first is the most important: A privately published book is created for the pleasure of the making. It is usually used as a gift, and its publisher does not expect to make any money on the work.

Private publishing can be as high- or as low-tech as you wish. If computers intimidate you, there are other ways to see your work in print.

HANDMADE BOOKS

There are lots of ways to create beautiful, one of a kind books to show off your creativity, and there are lots of books to show you how to do that. The one on my bookshelf is *Cover to Cover* by Shereen LaPlantz, and it's a good, basic text.

For purposes of this section, we're talking about making one original book that can then be replicated as often as you choose.

HAND-WRITE YOUR BOOK

This is the method used by all authors before Johannes Gutenberg invented a printing system for the mass production of books. It's simply pens, pencils, drawing supplies, and paper.

Oh, and a copy machine, either one you own or one that's located in your area.

Who chooses to publish books this way?

- Folks who want to make illustrated books to share with children—their own, their grandchildren, or their students.

- People who want to make family keepsakes to give as a gift for the holidays.

- Poets who collect their work in chapbooks to give away.

SUPPLIES

No matter what publishing method you choose, it is important to know how a book will be printed before you begin. This knowledge influences how you choose to design a book, what size to make it, whether it will be printed in color or black and white and a host of other factors. In this instance, your printer is a copy machine located in your home or at a local copy shop.

How does this knowledge impact your choice of supplies? The technology behind copy machines is the same as that used in scanners and digital cameras. Every time the light wand in a copy machine moves over an original document, it takes a picture of the original then transfers the image to a second piece of paper.

With this type of printing, what you see is what you get. In other words, whatever marks you make on your original document will be replicated on every subsequent copy.

Here are the best choices for the supplies you need to make your original document:

• Heavy, unlined, white paper. White card stock, available in most office supply stores, is a good choice. Its bright white won't interfere with your images, and it does not absorb too much ink so the edges of the marks you make stay crisp.

Except in very limited circumstances, it's not a good idea to use any color other than white as your paper choice in your original document. You can always copy your work onto color paper if you wish.

• Pens or markers with black ink. Just a bit of information here: over time, black ink fades far slower than any other color. Pencil fades more slowly than any ink.

• Pens or markers in color. If you wish to add color to your original documents, be sure to choose pens with sharp points so that the edges of any marks you make—whether it's an illustration or writing—are crisp and clear.

• Pencils to make light guidelines.

PRINTING CONSIDERATIONS

Unless you have access to a specialty copy machine, your work will be printed on paper in one of the following standard paper sizes:

8½ x 11 inches (letter size)
8½ x 14 inches (legal size and less commonly available)
11 x 17 inches (tabloid size)

You can, of course, have a copy shop cut paper to any size

you wish. Bear in mind that every time your copies are handled, the price of the result increases.

THE STEP-BY-STEP PROCESS

1. Plan what you will put on each page of your book. (You can download a PDF tutorial on how to plan a book at www.SonjaHakala.com.)

2. Visit your copy shop to determine if the plans for your book can be carried out on their printing equipment. Make adjustments to your book plan if necessary.

3. Write and/or draw each page of your book individually in the size it will be printed. Be sure to number the pages so your printer will know what comes first and what comes next. Remember that the person printing copies of your book will not read it to determine the order of the pages.

4. Deliver your originals to your printer. Ask them to create a proof copy for you to check.

5. Check your proof copy very, very carefully. Make any adjustments to your originals, if that will correct the problem. Be prepared to create new originals if necessary.

6. If you have made significant changes to your book, ask for a second proof copy. Check this carefully.

7. When you approve your proof, order the greatest number of copies you can afford at the time. The price per copy is usually less if you order in bulk than if you ask for one at a time.

8. Share your finished books with the world.

CHAPTER TWELVE

Typeset Your Own Books with Word Processing Software

IF YOU HAVE ACCESS to a computer, a printer, and word processing software such a Microsoft Word, you can typeset the interior of your book yourself.

One of the advantages of using this method is that you can, if you wish, print copies of your own book on your own printer. These copies can, in turn, be stapled or spirally bound with tools found in any good office supply store.

WORD PROCESSING ADVANTAGES AND LIMITATIONS

The advantages of using word processing software to typeset the interior of a book are obvious. This type of software is far less expensive than desktop publishing software. It's easier to learn. It's pretty common, so more people know something about how to use it.

But there are some very real limitations in using word processing software to typeset the interior of a book. First and foremost, this type of software was never meant to be used in this fashion. When compared to desktop publishing software such as Adobe's InDesign or Quark Xpress, you have far less control over the way text looks on a page in a word processing program. It is difficult to control such things as page numbers within sections or chapters, the space between lines of type (called leading), the size of a document, and the number of lines on a page of type.

And there can be very real compatibility issues between word processing documents and the printers used to manufacture books, especially when it comes to images and how fonts are handled. That's why you cannot make a cover in a word processing program

For these reasons, the most common complaint I hear about books typeset with word processing software is that they "don't look like real books." That's why I do not recommend using word processing software to create a high-end book-on-paper that you hope to sell in bookstores. But for private publishing purposes, word processing software can truly fit the bill.

FORMATTING TEXT WITH WORD PROCESSING SOFTWARE

Just to be clear, in book publishing the terms formatting and typesetting both refer to the way text and images appear on a page. Formatting has everything to do with the way a book looks on paper.

Here are some examples of the formatting choices I made on this page. The indent of this paragraph is .25 inches. The width of this column of type is 4.25 inches wide by 7 inches high. The size of this font, which is Century Schoolbook by the way, is 11 points. There are 3 points of leading. Leading is the space between the bottom of one line of type and the top of the next line of type. All of these choices were made to ensure the text's legibility.

Each of these factors can be controlled to a very minute degree with a desktop publishing program such as Adobe InDesign or Quark Xpress. There's a whole section devoted to the finer points of interior design starting on page 63 but for now, just be aware that the quality of your reading experience with this book is dependent to a certain degree on the text design choices you see on every page.

FORMATTING TIPS FOR WORD PROCESSING SOFTWARE

For many people, a word processing program and a computer are just high-tech substitutes for a typewriter. Nothing could be further from the truth.

Here are the most common mistakes folks make when using word processing software to format a book, and how to avoid them.

NEVER USE TWO SPACES AFTER PUNCTUATION

The main difference between a typewriter and a computer is that a typewriter is a mechanical device and subject to mechanical constraints. A computer, on the other hand, works by a very different set of rules. When you type on a typewriter, every letter takes up the same amount of space. This every-character-is-equal-to-all-others fact of life is called monotype. It means that the small letter i is allotted the same amount of paper as the capital letter W. Of course, they are hardly the same size at all.

The mechanical necessity of monotype spacing is the reason why folks taught to keyboard on a typewriter put two spaces after a period. If they didn't, the spaces between sentences would look the same as the spaces between words.

A computer automatically adjusts the spacing of a line of text to fit the letters in it. When you use a computer and word processing software, this combination of technologies automatically adjusts the spacing after a period so that our eyes pick up this key bit of information.

Take a moment to look at the three preceding paragraphs. Note how much the double spaces after each period jump out at you visually.

Putting two spaces after a period—or any punctuation mark—often betrays the amateur status of a writer to a traditional publisher. If you intend to submit your work to an agent or traditional publisher or a magazine or newspaper editor, be sure you use only one space at a time.

NEVER USE THE TAB KEY—FOR ANYTHING

This paragraph was indented with the tab key.

This line was centered with the tab key.

Why not use the tab key to indent a paragraph or adjust the location of a line of type? Because different programs interpret the spacing of a tab key in different ways.

If you create a word processing document with tabs, then send it to a printer, the software used by the printer will probably interpret your tabs in such a way that your lines of type end up looking something like this:

A line of type indented with a tab key can cause strange alignments such as this one.

Also, tabs in word processing documents can leave gaping holes   in text when it is imported into   a desktop publishing program. If you   decide to use a professional book designer,   she or he will have to manually take out all of your tabs.

So how do you indent paragraphs? Most word processing programs allow their users to set the formatting so that paragraph indents happen automatically when you hit RETURN on your keyboard. Let me give you an example using Microsoft Word since it's the most commonly used word processing software program.

When the program is open, you will see a menu across the top of your screen that reads:

Word File Edit View Insert Format Font, etc.

Click on Format and a menu drops down with sub-menus in it. The second sub-menu is titled "Paragraph" and within it, you'll find another called "Indentation." There's a choice marked "Special" with a lozenge-shaped button under it that looks something like what you see on the next page:

(none) ↕

Those up and down arrows indicate there are choices to be made here. Click on one of the arrows and another short menu drops down with the choices "First Line" and "Hanging". To set a paragraph indent, choose "First Line" as in the first line of a paragraph. When you do, the blank rectangle to the right of "First Line" is automatically filled with the measurement .5".

If you do nothing more, your automatic paragraph indent will be one-half inch. This means that every time you hit your return key, the next line of text will automatically indent by the amount you specify. You can leave this measurement at .5" if you wish or change it to another measurement by changing the measurement in this box.

You also use the Paragraph features of the Format menu to control the spacing between lines of type. Take the time to learn this area of your word processing program so you can avoid using your TAB key.

DO NOT USE THE SPACE BAR ON YOUR KEYBOARD TO INDENT LINES OF TYPE

DO NOT HIT THE RETURN KEY TWICE IN A ROW TO MAKE SPACES BETWEEN YOUR PARAGRAPHS

As you have probably gathered, aligning and spacing text on a page is a large part of formatting. The reasons for not using your SPACE bar or RETURN key to create extra space are the same as those for not using the TAB key.

Both of these situations—centering text or creating spaces between paragraphs—can be controlled through the same "Paragraph" menu described in the previous section on TABS. If you need more assistance, please consult the HELP section of your word processing program.

DO NOT OVERUSE CAPITALIZATION, QUOTATION MARKS, BOLD OR ITALIC TYPE

There's a **general** rule in good typography that goes something like this: If a reader becomes aware of the way words look on a page, you've *lost* the reader. In a novel, this **awareness** can jolt a *reader* right out of a key scene. In nonfiction, too many interruptions make a Reader's attention jump from **one point** to another, and the "author's desire" to lead the reader to what is most important is thwarted.

What interrupts a reader's attention? Misspellings, missing words, misused words (its and it's being the most common), and typographical flourishes like the boldface, capitalization, quotation marks, and italics in the first paragraph of this section. Every time you use one of these flourishes, you demand of your reader "Look at this! Look at this!" If you flourish too much, your text becomes irritating and difficult to read. With so many books to choose from, why would a reader choose one that's irritating and difficult to read over one that is not?

For more information on this topic, please consult the section on interior design starting on page 63.

CHAPTER THIRTEEN

Publishing Path Three:
Self-Publishing

THE KEY DIFFERENCE between independent publishers and self-publishers is readily apparent in the quality of the final product. Independent publishers take on all the responsibilities of traditional publishing companies in the production of a book, making sure it is well edited and designed. Consequently, a reader cannot tell the difference between a traditionally published book and an independently published book.

In self-publishing, however, quality is a vague concept.

VANITY PUBLISHING/SELF-PUBLISHING

If you do an internet search on the term "self publishing," you'll find a raft of companies offering to help authors publish their own books. In reality, the overwhelming majority of companies that market themselves as "self-publishers" are vanity publishers with a new name.

Before digital technology, writers who chose to use vanity publishers were forced, because of the demands of offset printing, to purchase a thousand copies or more of their book. Now with digital printing, authors don't have to buy a thousand copies. But this is the only difference between a company that calls itself a "self-publisher" and a vanity press.

Companies involved in vanity publishing do not distinguish between low-quality and high-quality books. In fact, vanity presses are not in business because they care about the quality of an author's writing at all. Vanity publishing companies make their money by charging fees for their services, and then selling books to their main customers, book authors.

Vanity publishing companies don't expect to make money on book sales to the general public, and they are generally not disappointed. Yes, I know they tout extraordinary success stories on the home pages of their websites. But they are the true exceptions to the rule—if they are true.

Most vanity presses advertise low-priced package plans if you publish with them. (Be sure to check out the next chapter for an overview of the marketing lingo common among self-publishing companies.) Once an author is enticed by these low prices, the company then uses a number of aggressive marketing techniques to up-sell and cross-sell additional or enhanced services so that the low-priced package plan is no longer low.

You should be aware that most bookstores and libraries are very reluctant to buy books published by the better-known vanity presses such as iUniverse, XLibris, Trafford, and Author House. When the first of these presses began publishing books in the late 1990s, bookstores quickly realized that readers wouldn't buy them because their quality was so poor, and that attitude is still pretty much the norm.

By the way, Author House, XLibris, Trafford Publishing, and iUniverse are all part of a company called Author Solutions. Author Solutions is, in turn, owned by a private equity firm called Bertram Capital Management.

Since these vanity presses were the first to use print-on-demand technology, that technology—and its name—became associated with this form of publishing and got a pretty bad rap because of it. But print-on-demand technology is used by many traditional and independent publishers nowadays, including the publisher of this book. (See the definition of print-on-demand below.)

Generally, vanity presses set the retail price of a book, and then charge its author a percentage of that price—sometimes as high as 90 percent—for copies. In other words, if a vanity press sets a $20 retail price on a book, its author could pay as much as $18 a copy for it.

To put this in perspective, Amazon.com generally discounts books with a retail price of more than $10 by 30 percent. So if our vanity press author's $20 book is available on Amazon, he or she could get copies cheaper there ($14) than with their own publisher. (It's normal for authors to receive a certain number of free copies of their books from traditional publishers, and are able to purchase additional copies for 40 to 50 percent off of their book's retail price.)

Buying copies of your own book from a vanity publisher after you've already paid the costs for editing, design, typesetting, and printing is no bargain, in my estimation.

There are some good reasons to consider using a vanity press but they are limited. If you require only a small number of books (often referred to as a short-run project), then I would recommend using a company such as Blurb.com that supplies online software with which you can create your own book. By the way, Blurb.com authors retain all of the rights to their books. (See the term RIGHTS in the Business Concept section of the glossary for a complete explanation of what this means.) Many self-publishing company contracts take all of an author's rights to her or his work. And as Michael Finerman so clearly points out in his very good book *The Fine Print*, it is very, very difficult to get those rights back once they are gone.

PRINT-ON-DEMAND

I know I'm repeating this but it's worth emphasizing. Print-on-demand is another name for digital print technology. This way of printing is now used by traditional publishers as well as independent and vanity publishers. When an order is placed for a print-on-demand book, the whole work is printed, paginated, and bound in a cover in minutes, and it doesn't matter who's publishing it.

IF YOU DECIDE TO USE A SELF-PUBLISHING COMPANY

If you decide to explore this publishing path, please use caution when sharing your personal information. I've worked with a number of authors who shared their personal information with self-publishing companies, and they were hounded by salespeople after their initial contact. Also note that some self-publishing companies will not reveal their charges for services until you sign an agreement with them for publishing your book. Please do not agree to or sign anything until you know all of the costs involved, and after all of your questions have been answered.

As I noted earlier, I've been involved in book marketing for some time and also provide services for independent publishers through my own company, Full Circle Press LLC. Taking that background into consideration, I have to tell you that I am in awe of the marketing materials put out by self-publishing companies, which is why I wrote the following chapter. Some companies tout paid services that are actually free if you independently publish your book. Some of them use slight shades of meaning or unfamiliar terms to give the appearance of offering hefty publishing packages that are little more than the smoke and mirrors favored by the Wizard of Oz.

Always bear in mind that your excitement over finishing your book and your desire to see it in print make you vulnerable when you need to be at your most hardheaded. If you decide to explore the self-publishing route, read the next chapter carefully to make sure you spend your money wisely.

CHAPTER FOURTEEN

What Are Self-Publishing Companies Really Selling?

ACCORDING TO R.R. BOWKER, the company responsible for publishing *Books in Print* and for assigning ISBNs in the U.S., the number of self-published titles in 2009 topped 764,000. By contrast, the number of titles published through traditional companies fell to 289,729.

In that year, Lulu.com produced 10,386 titles while two divisions of Author Solutions—XLibris and AuthorHouse—brought out 19,606 titles between them while Amazon's CreateSpace published another 21,819 titles. Another company, BiblioBazaar, put out an astounding 272,930 titles, all works in the public domain. (In other words, no living authors need apply to BiblioBazaar.)

As jaw dropping as these numbers are, there's nothing in them to tell you what the authors of books published by CreateSpace or XLibris sold. And as far as I know, there's no reliable source for those numbers.

The lesson I'm trying to teach you by flinging these statistics in your direction is that it's always a good idea to dig beneath the surface when presented with any numbers in book publishing. The questions to ask yourself when dealing with a self-publishing company are: What are the odds you will recoup the money you spend on publishing services through book sales, and how important is that to you?

Self-publishing companies function something like traditional publishers in that they are one-stop shops for everything a book needs from editing to text design to distribution and printing. You tell them what you want, and they provide it for a fee. For folks who feel overwhelmed by the idea of independently publishing their own work, a self-publishing company feels safe. And that's fine. What works for person A is not necessarily the right choice for person B. My job in this chapter is to make sure you know exactly what a self-publishing company is offering to do for you so you know what you're getting for your money.

The following list of author services was compiled from the packages commonly offered by the bigger self-publishing companies. Accompanying each item is a brief description of what the marketing term really means, and what the service actually entails.

• DISCOUNTED AUTHOR SUPPORT SERVICES

The whole purpose of a self-publishing company is author support services. These services can include: Assignment of an ISBN number, editing, interior and cover design, typesetting, author corrections, distribution, marketing, sales, and the payment of royalties.

When you see an item in a publishing package with this sort of description, you need to specifically ask the company how they define support services, and in what depth these support services are provided.

For example, in traditional or independent publishing circles, distribution and sales means the hiring of a company to deliver books to customers, and keep track of what is bought and what is returned. In a self-publishing company, these same terms may mean nothing more than having your book for sale on the self-publishing company's website. If this is the case, your book will not be available anywhere except on the website or from sales that you make directly. If you want it to be on Amazon, for example, you will be responsible for getting it there.

If a company claims that this part of their publishing package includes editing, make sure it's more than running your manuscript through a spell check.

The phrase "author support services" is a vague term used to cover a multitude of meanings. If you start negotiations with a self-publishing company that uses this terminology, my advice is to be very clear about what you know your book needs, and be certain to get a printed copy of what a company promises to provide.

And if they use the word discounted in this phrase, be sure to ask what the cost of their services is discounted from.

• **EDITORIAL REVIEW**

In most cases, authors think of an editorial review as a hands-on, in-the-trenches look at a raw manuscript by a professional editor who actually reads the material. A review, under these circumstances, could include advice on how to organize a book for more cohesion, pinpointing plot or character development weaknesses in a work of fiction, or making suggestions for additions.

A review of this kind takes time—anywhere from four to eight hours to read a manuscript with the same amount of time dedicated to writing a review. A professional book editor charges anywhere from $250 to $1,000 for such work with an average of $500. So how in the world could a self-publishing company give this service away for free?

They don't. A self-publishing company wants to entice you to be one of their authors. Their profit lies in the sale of services and books to authors. Do you really think they would tell an author something negative about her or his manuscript?

Nope, me neither.

When this service is listed in a publishing package, it

most often means someone at the company sends you a form email or letter to say your book is suitable for publication. If you're truly interested in producing a quality book, that's not news you can use.

FORMAT TEMPLATES

For those of you who have never used graphic design software, think of a template as a gelatin mold. No matter what color gelatin you pour into it, the result looks the same.

Software programs such as Microsoft Word use templates to aid users in the creation of brochures or business forms such as invoices or letterheads, and they are a great help. A format template for a book, however, eliminates the need for individually designing a cover or interior.

Using a template saves a great deal of time and money— for the self-publishing company. There's no need to retain the services of a designer, no need to consider the needs of an individual book. And once a template is set up, it can be used ad infinitum with no additional expense to the company.

If you have an image of how your book ought to look, a format template is not the way to go.

COMPETITIVE PRICING ANALYSIS

This phrase is one of my favorites because it sounds so professional, as if you need special expertise to do this sort of work. But as discussed in the chapter on marketing, you can do this easily yourself with a trip online to Amazon.com to see what other books cost that are in the same niche as yours.

In practice, self-publishing companies base their retail prices on the cost of printing your book plus their profit, and not much more. To understand this calculus for yourself, please turn to Chapter Ten, page 99, on publishing math. Then drop by Amazon.com to check out the prices of books similar to yours. There, you've done your own competitive pricing analysis.

COPYRIGHT INFORMATION PERSONALIZATION

I always scratch my head in wonderment when I see this phrase because there's no way to personalize copyright information—it's the same for everyone who publishes a book in the United States.

In a nutshell, as soon as you write something, it is yours. You own the copyright. In fact, you and your heirs own the copyright to everything you write because it extends for 75 years after your death. A quick bit of research on www.copyright.gov will give you every bit of information you need on this subject.

PREPARATION OF FINAL PROOF

I have mixed feelings about this item when it appears in a publishing package. On the one hand, every author who pays to have her or his book published has the absolute right to see a final proof copy of the entire book—including cover—before it is sent to a printer. So this item should be part of every publishing package as a matter of course.

So I'm reassured when I see this listing.

On the other hand, listing this item individually strikes me as a bit of marketing hype, a way to bulk out a package so it seems more than it is.

My advice: If you don't see this item specifically listed, ask to be sure it is part of what you buy. If seeing and approving the final proof of a book you're paying for is not included in a publishing package, look for another company with which to do business.

ONE ROUND OF AUTHOR CORRECTIONS

Of all the sticky wickets strewn about the path to publishing, this is one of the stickiest. First let me explain what I mean by the phrase "author corrections".

In traditional publishing, authors usually see their books twice while they're in progress so that they can make corrections. The first time occurs while the book is still in manuscript form after it's been copyedited. At this point, any substantial changes should be made to the book.

The second time for corrections occurs after a book has been typeset at a moment conventionally referred to as "first pages." A set of first pages is given to the author as well as to a proofreader so that both can catch last minute spelling mistakes as well as check the work of the typesetter. In other words, this is the moment for catching the last, small mistakes before they are set in print.

Since the author does not pay for this service in traditional publishing, there is no limit to the number of corrections she or he can make. This is not so when you purchase a package of services from a self-publishing company.

In this scenario, author corrections refers to the first pages stage of the publishing process, and the way they are handled differs widely from company to company. Some companies stipulate a set number of author corrections in their publishing packages. When that number is reached, authors are charged per correction. And the definition of "author correction" varies as well. A misspelling or an absent comma is usually considered an author correction. But if you want to rewrite a paragraph, this may be outside the acceptable norm for an author correction, and you'll be charged for the change. Mistakes made by the computer doing the template formatting of your book may be counted as "author corrections" if you ask to have them fixed. In other words, you can end up paying for mistakes that someone else introduced into your work.

My advice in this area is as follows: When negotiating an agreement with a self-publishing company, find out what constitutes an author correction. Ask if there is a limit to how many you can make. What if there is an error made during the typesetting phase? Will you be charged for that? You'd be surprised how quickly the cost of making corrections to a manuscript adds up, so be sure you know what this part of a self-publishing company's services entails.

FULL COLOR COVER

This is marketing hype. All the digital printers used by self-publishing companies print covers in color. There are no black-and-white-only digital cover printers. This is automatically part of every publishing package because of the technology involved.

ISBN ALLOCATION AND ADMINISTRATION

This is another bit of marketing hype. In order for a self-publishing company to track inventory within the book publishing industry, they need to put an ISBN on your book.

Because of their volume, self-publishing companies purchase ISBNs in blocks of a thousand. This means they are paying $1.75 per ISBN.

When you purchase a block of ISBNs (which is covered in depth on page 34), you receive a digital file listing all of your numbers. Allocating an ISBN is as simple as assigning your next available number to the next book.

Always remember that ISBNs are assigned to publishing companies, not authors. They function as a book's social security number, and the profit from sales follows the ISBN trail. In other words, the holder of the ISBN controls the money flow, and the division of profits.

My advice in this area is to find a self-publishing company that allows you to use your own ISBN. Blurb, Lulu, and CreateSpace all have an option for an author to use her or his own ISBN. That way, everyone's clear about who owns the right to publish your book.

ISBN BARCODE CREATION

Another bit of marketing hype. ISBN barcodes can be purchased along with ISBN numbers. No publishing company has to create them, and several printers include this service for free to their customers.

LIBRARY OF CONGRESS CATALOGING

The Library of Congress (LOC) provides a free cataloging

service to most book publishers. This cataloging information, which appears on the copyright page of a book, is used by librarians to find just the right spot on their shelves for a book. This is particularly important for non-fiction books.

The LOC also retains a copy of every book they catalog. Sounds like a good deal, doesn't it?

It is. But let me give you a few more details.

Librarians appreciate and they do use the LOC cataloging information. But if a library wishes to purchase a book, the appearance or non-appearance of LOC information will not impact that decision. The premise in publishing circles, one promoted by self-publishing companies, is that the presence of LOC cataloging information enhances your book's sales potential but in fact, there is no evidence that this is true.

For more information on cataloging, please see the Publishers Cataloging-in-Publication entry in the Glossary on page 180.

QUARTERLY SALES REPORTS/QUARTERLY ROYALTY REPORTS

I've never been sure why these two items (often listed separately) appear in so many publishing packages. Industry-wide, book publishing works on a quarterly basis.

For example, I receive sales payments from my distributor (Ingram) for this book 90 days (a quarter) after the sale is complete. Why? Because of returns. Booksellers (including online booksellers) have 90 days in which to return unsold books to their publisher for full credit. So distributors withhold payment until this 90-day period has passed.

BULK DISCOUNT FOR ORDERS OVER 50 COPIES

Most digital printers give their clients a small break in the costs of bulk printing, and 50 copies is usually the lowest quantity for this. Depending on the printer, there could be another price break at 100 copies and another at 250.

In general, self-publishing companies charge their clients a high percentage of a book's retail price for copies, somewhere in the neighborhood of 75 to 90 percent. If the self-publishing company in question is akin to Blurb.com, for example, doing business this way makes sense because Blurb provides free software so that anyone can design their own books. In other words, a company like Blurb could not exist if it did not make money on its printing.

I make a clear distinction between companies that provide just printing services and companies such as iUniverse or XLibris that provide author services. These latter companies earn their daily bread by charging for editorial services, graphic design, marketing, etc. They make their profit by charging higher-than-necessary prices to an author for copies of his or her book. Under this scenario, it becomes difficult for an author to recoup the expenses of publishing through hand-selling copies of his or her book.

This is a long way of telling you that the break you get when you order 50 copies of your book from a self-publishing company isn't that much of a break. For more on this, please see the chapter on publishing math on page 99.

FIVE FREE COPIES

How much does it cost for a self-publishing company to print five copies of a book with 120 to 200 pages, a color cover, and a black & white interior? About $20. Even with shipping, the total value of this benefit is $30 at the most.

You should know that most traditional publishers provide a minimum of 20 free copies—often more than that—to their authors. Believe me, when you see this benefit listed in a package from a self-publishing company, there's nothing free about these five copies. They are the way that self-publishing companies encourage authors—their principle consumers—to buy books. After all, what author could resist ordering more copies after receiving the initial five?

CHAPTER FIFTEEN

If You Decide to Use a Self-Publishing Company: A Few Recommendations

REMEMBER HOW I ASKED you some key questions at the beginning of this book? If you decide to look into self-publishing companies that provide author services, my primary recommendation is to go back and read your answers before you do anything else. Your answers to the questions at the beginning of this book are your guiding principles as you search for the right self-publishing partner.

Here are some additional questions and guidance to help you with your search.

1. Do you want your book to be available for bookstore sales?

If your answer to this question is yes, you want to know if a self-publishing company can distribute your book to bookstores at the standard trade discount with returns, the bookstore standard. What is the cost of this service?

2. Do you want your book available through online booksellers in addition to the self-publishing company?

If yes, you need to find out if the company in question can do this for you or not. If you have to send books to Amazon yourself, what will the self-publishing company charge you for copies of your book? Does that price leave you a profit?

3. Are you prepared to sell your rights to your work to a self-publishing company?

According to author Michael Finerman in *The Fine Print*, the larger self-publishing companies have contracts in which authors agree to give up nearly all rights to their work, including audio and electronic rights. Be advised that there are a growing number of self-publishing companies, such as Amazon's CreateSpace, that don't force an author to sign an exclusive publishing contract.

4. What author services do you really need?

If you want to create a book just for family and friends, you probably don't need editorial services. And if you use free design software on a site like Blurb.com, you don't need a designer for your cover or interior either. If you simply want to have your book available for download, you can use Microsoft Word to create a document you can sell in Amazon's Kindle store. (By the way, there is free software available on Amazon that allows other-than-Kindle owners to purchase electronic books from the Kindle store.)

If you want editorial and graphic-design services, will a self-publishing company deliver what you seek?

Duplicating the quality of the products from traditional book publishers—the gold standard in the industry—can be done by you as an independent publisher with some applied effort. So before you bet your wallet on a self-publishing company with author services, take the time to read the chapters on independent publishing starting on page 33. There are some narrow circumstances (see the chapter on private publishing starting on page 119 for the best examples of this) under which a self-publishing company may be the best choice for your work. I just want you to be sure.

CHAPTER SIXTEEN

Publishing Path Four: Traditional Publishing

DID YOU KNOW?

• Most new titles published by traditional publishing companies sell fewer than 1,000 copies.

• More than 60 percent of the books published by traditional publishing houses do not earn back their author's advances.

• Of every ten titles published by a traditional publisher, six lose money, two break even, one shows some profit, and if the publisher is lucky, one makes a lot of money.

• According to agents, the most difficult book to sell is the second book by an author who did not earn back his or her advance. Remember it's the publisher who determines the amount of an author's advance, and the size of a print run so the bar in this scenario is set by the publisher, not the author. In most cases, the author does most of the marketing work.

• If the editor who acquires a book leaves the publishing company before the book is completed, it is quite likely that the publishing company will never print the book. Orphaned books are common in traditional publishing.

• Traditional publishing companies accept fewer than 10 percent of the manuscripts offered to them by agents.

• Of the more than 1.2 million individual titles for sale in the U.S. in 2008, only ten sold more than a million copies each.

• The *New York Times* bestseller list is not an accurate reflection of sales despite the newspaper's claims to the contrary. The list can be manipulated by planting buyers in bookstores to purchase copies of new titles on certain days in order to secure bragging rights and attention for the publishing house and author. There are consultants who make a comfortable living orchestrating what appears on the bestseller list.

Actions taken by the *Times* can also skew the results. For example, the newspaper did not record the sales of electronic books until 2011. And after sales of the *Harry Potter* books made them the dominant titles on the fiction list, the *Times* ruled they were children's books and therefore not eligible for inclusion on the bestseller list.

• Of all the titles published each year, approximately 15 percent are fiction. That's more than 60,000 new novels or collections of short stories on the market every year.

TRADITIONAL PUBLISHING: A FEW WORDS OF ADVICE

For many authors, there's nothing quite like the thrill of having a book accepted by a traditional publishing company. The most common feeling can be summed up in the phrase "I've made it!"

Now I would never disparage that thrill. I've experienced it myself, three times. But I've played counselor to too many sad authors not to realize that this route is not for everyone.

Most of the eternal difficulties between authors and publishers come under the heading of unfulfilled expectations. Authors, especially first-timers, believe their publisher is just as excited about their book as they are. But publishers operate on a raft mentality—the more books they float, the greater the odds that some of them will turn a profit. Authors tend to see themselves as one-person kayaks.

If you decide to pursue this path to publishing, my advice here is the same as it is for publishing independently or with a self-publishing company. Writers on the brink of publication are vulnerable, and the very real excitement of achieving a personal dream can and does overwhelm common sense just when common sense is most needed.

You must be as practical in traditional publishing as you should be if you choose a different path.

If you have dreams of making money as a book author with a traditional publisher, you need to know that that is a very rare occurrence. There's a reason why the names James Patterson, Sue Grafton, Stephen King, or J.K. Rowling are so familiar. They are rare birds in the industry.

What about the thousands of writers you never hear about? Should they be considered successful or unsuccessful? I think it all depends on how you define success.

A doctor who lives in my area once approached me about ghostwriting a book for him. After some wonderful conversations together, I persuaded him to do the book with the assistance of his wife, a poet.

They did work together, quite successfully. The result of their efforts was accepted by a large, traditional publisher, and very well reviewed. A couple of years later, during an email exchange, I asked him how the book was selling. "Oh, my publisher sends me royalty statements, and I put them in a drawer unopened," he said. But he went on to tell me that the best part about being published was the credibility his book conferred. That credibility translated into lots of speaking engagements in his field.

To my mind, that's one of the best way to look at book publishing, as an adjunct to what you already do.

ADVANTAGES OF TRADITIONAL PUBLISHING

• Someone else hires and pays for editing, design, and printing.

• Someone else handles distribution and sales.

• Someone else handles some of the marketing.

• Bragging rights. Traditional publishers accept only one out of ten book projects offered to them by agents.

• Authors are paid an advance on their royalties upon acceptance of their books.

DISADVANTAGES OF TRADITIONAL PUBLISHING

• Someone other than you makes the final decision about your book's retail price.

• Unless you are dealing with a specialty publisher—one that works in a particular niche—your book may never be offered for sale in places where your target market can find it.

• Most authors never recoup the advances paid to them by their publishers. In other words, the advance is all the money they ever see. Advances in traditional publishing have been steadily shrinking since 2000. For years, the lowest advance offered by a publisher was $1,000. Nowadays, a $500 advance is common.

• Authors are forbidden by contract from selling copies of their own books in certain venues, bookstores and libraries being chief among them.

• The author's portion of the retail price of every book sold (the royalty rate) rarely reaches one dollar per copy.

• Most publishers work exclusively with agents and rarely accept unagented books. Agents make their commissions (15 to 20 percent of everything an author earns) before the author is paid. In other words, a publisher pays the agent who, in turn, pays the author.

• Most marketing efforts need to be undertaken by the author, mostly at the author's expense. In other words, the marketing efforts of a traditionally published author are the same as those made by an independently publishing author.

WHAT ARE THE ODDS?

From the end of World War II up to the most recent economic downturn, the number of books accepted for publication by traditional companies grew at a steady pace. (The number of books published by traditional companies has been decreasing since 2008.) But as the number of titles accepted increased so has the number of writers who wish to be published. As a result, the ratio of acceptances to rejections has remained fairly steady at 10 to 15 percent acceptances to 85 to 90 percent rejections.

Now a one-in-ten chance of having your book accepted definitely beats the odds of winning the lottery. But like so many numbers in publishing, the statement of those odds is somewhat deceptive. Why? Because the number of hurdles between writers and publishers has increased.

When Theodore Geisel (Dr. Seuss) published his first book in 1937, *And to Think That I Saw It on Mulberry Street*, he shopped his manuscript to 27 publishers. If he were to shop the same book nowadays, he'd be sending it out to 27 agents, not publishers.

Even though literary agents have been part of publishing since 1880, chances are pretty good that Dr. Seuss mailed or presented his first manuscript directly to the editors and publishers he hoped would accept his work. Book publishing at that time was a clubby industry centered in New York City. If you wanted to get published, NYC was the only place to be.

By the time Seuss published *The Cat in the Hat* in 1957, would-be authors without direct connections to publishing companies in New York most often submitted their full manuscripts to a review by publishing employees called "first readers." These folks, mainly young women who were recent college graduates, plowed through the manuscripts in the slush pile searching for the few worth publishing.

If the truth be told, every agent and editor I know reports that the overwhelming majority of submissions is not of publishable quality so the expense of maintaining a slush pile doesn't make economic sense. That's why most publishers no longer accept unagented books. Why should they pay someone to read manuscripts when they can get agents to do it for them for free? After all, agents are paid by authors.

And that statistic I cited at the beginning of this section, about publishers accepting only 10 to 15 percent of everything that's submitted to them? That's 10 to 15 percent of what's submitted to them by agents who have already rejected 85 to 90 percent of what's been submitted to them. That makes the odds against being traditionally published much higher.

A BUSINESS ATTITUDE ENHANCES THE CHANCES

Throughout this book, I've emphasized the fact that writing is an art and a craft while publishing is a business. In my experience, the most successful authors are the ones who not only understand that attitude but embrace it. How do you convey that to an agent and publisher? By producing a professional book proposal that you market to a carefully targeted group of folks most interested in your work.

Agents and publishers reject most books for two reasons— bad writing and bad marketing. I have to admit that after 25 years in the publishing business, the anti-marketing behavior of authors still baffles me. But I've seen novelists send their manuscripts to how-to-only book publishers. I've seen political screeds end up at poetry-only houses. I know agents who explicitly refuse to represent romance novels who routinely receive manuscripts from romance novelists.

Marketing a book proposal follows exactly the same procedure as marketing a book. (See Chapter Nine, page 81.) You do the research to find your target market, and then you create the materials that will most interest that market.

Agents and publishers handle author submissions in a way that makes sense to them, and meeting their specifications is the mark of a professional author. The best place to start your research is the *Literary Marketplace* which you can find on paper in larger public and university libraries or on the web at www.LiteraryMarketplace.com. A seven-day subscription (currently $19.95) gives you access to the best database of publishers and agents that you will find.

Read the *LMP* listings carefully, and compile a list of agents and the few publishers who still accept unagented manuscripts in your book's subject area. With that list in hand, do an online search on every agent and company you chose. Pay close attention to how materials must be submitted and what information must be included. And strictly adhere to those guidelines.

WHO IS THE RIGHT PUBLISHER FOR YOUR BOOK

I think it's just as important for writers to be choosy about their publishers as publishers are about writers. What's my criterion? In two words, marketing acumen.

I've emphasized throughout this book that it's important for writers to pinpoint and understand the niche where their book belongs. We use the term readers as a collective noun but all you have to do is take a look at any reader's bookshelf or Kindle list to know we are all quite specific in our tastes in books.

So are publishers. If you scratch the surface of most big publishers (those that produce 100+ titles a year), you'll find subcategories within. Certain editors handle certain types of books, and nothing else. There can be imprints (think of this as departments within a book publishing company) set up for the exlusive handling of mystery novels or travel guides or self-help titles.

This specificity is usually quite apparent in small- to mid-sized publishers because these smaller companies are dedicated to one subject matter or type of book. Let me give you a few examples of what I mean.

Wiley Publishing (www.Wiley.com) is a great example

of a large company that functions as a group of smaller companies. I've published two how-to quilt books with Wiley in their *Teach Yourself Visually* series, so I can tell you from experience that their staff is well-trained and pragmatic. They have well-honed systems in place for book production, and they listen to their authors' marketing suggestions.

If you visit their home page, you'll note that the company lists 23 subject categories to guide visitors to their book offerings. Wiley also maintains imprints such as the ubiquitous *For Dummies* series and *Frommer's* travel books. If the subject matter of your book (they handle only non-fiction) fits one of their categories, they would be a good partner to explore because of their pragmatic orientation to publishing.

My second example is **Aspire Media**, the parent company of **Interweave** (www.Interweave.com). Its target market is the arts and crafts enthusiast, a huge audience by anyone's reckoning. (It is estimated there are 21 million quilters in the U.S., just to give you an idea of the size.)

Aspire's Interweave, which it acquired in 2005, is a marketing juggernaut. Not only do they publish books, they publish 16 magazines, ebooks, video products, three television shows, national craft events, and they maintain a formidable online presence.

If you are an author of an appropriate book, Interweave's marketing prowess would be a terrific asset. Believe me, they do far more than send out review copies of books.

My third example is **Poisoned Pen Press**, an independent publisher that grew out of a bookstore by the same name (www.PoisonedPen Press.com). They publish mysteries, and their marketing strategy is based on their experience as booksellers, an on-the-ground view, if you will.

They are one of the few publishers that still accepts non-agented books, and their criteria for submissions are quite specific. If you have a mystery to sell that fits their niche, they would be a good partner in your venture.

Based on my experience with a number of writers and the

feedback I hear at my workshops, the number one complaint of dissatisfied authors in traditional publishing is the lack of marketing from their publisher. That's why I urge you to focus your inquiries about publication on companies that will help you enhance your position as a published author.

WHAT GOES INTO A GOOD BOOK PROPOSAL?

As I noted above, every publisher and agent wants to see certain items in book proposals. Agents often submit books to the same set of editors, and over time, they've learned what those editors like. (This is especially true in children's books.) Therefore, a good book proposal from you enhances their chances (and yours) of making a sale.

That being said, the following list generally follows what most agents and publishers seek. One more caveat: Spend the money to have your proposal and any book excerpt professionally edited by someone with book experience. When you start to do your research into agents and publishers, you'll find that many of them recommend this.

THE PARTS OF A BOOK PROPOSAL

Overview: This introductory section must be as succinct as possible. You need to convey the gist of your book, and its general market. If you are selling a novel, this section will be a tightly written synopsis of your book.

Target market description: What is the prospective market for this book? What are the sales possibilities? Get some numbers in this section, especially if your work is non-fiction. In other words, describe your readership.

Product description: How many pages (approximately) will your book have? What dimensions? Will your book include images or maps? How about appendices or a bibliography? Include everything that impacts the cost of producing your book.

Comparative title analysis: See page 88 for a full

description of how to do this. The goal of this part of your book proposal is to explain to an agent or publisher how your work is like others in the same area and how it is better or different. Include the retail prices and descriptions of other books in your category.

Suggested table of contents (non-fiction): Publishers and agents want to be sure you've thought your book through. What are you going to include?

Excerpt (fiction, short story, essay) or **Sample chapter** (non-fiction): You must show publishers and agents that you are an accomplished writer. They will not spend money polishing your prose. Strut your best stuff and have it edited before you send it out. A note here: There are times when an agent realizes that a book is "almost there." If that is the case, they may recommend that you spend the money to have your book polished before they accept it. If that happens to you, ask for recommendations for editors.

Suggested marketing plan: What are you currently doing to market yourself? Are you a well-known blogger in your field? Do you maintain a website dedicated to your subject area? Are you a speaker at conferences? In addition, if your book is published, what do you personally plan to do to market it? This is a very important area, one that gets a lot of attention from agents and publishers. Remember, most publishers do little marketing other than send out review copies. If you're not willing to market yourself and your work, they probably won't be interested in taking the financial risk of producing your book.

Author biography: Who are you? What is your educational experience in your field? Have you been published before? Of all the places where you can show a prospective agent or publisher that you are a professional, this is the one that probably matters most. Why? Because agents and publishers, even if they don't talk about it openly, look for pragmatic, experienced people with whom they can work.

Inexperienced authors or those who believe that the world is holding its breath waiting for their books are more expensive to work with than folks who understand that publishing is a business. Needy authors are viewed as time sinks and avoided when possible no matter how good their writing may be. Egos take time to massage, and folks in traditional publishing houses (who work very hard in an industry that is not replete with monetary rewards) don't have time for handling artistic temperament.

Think of it this way: A book proposal is a job application. You are, in essence, asking a company to invest in you and your product. You are asking them to take a risk by accepting your work because if your book succeeds, they make money. Your goal in a book proposal it to convince an agent or publisher that you have something they want *and* that you are the right person to deliver it.

ONE NOTE OF CAUTION

Please be aware there's a growing trend among a small number of tiny publishing companies to act as though they are traditional when they are not. This works in a number of ways. In the best-case scenario, a publisher is up front about who pays for what before contracts are signed. This gives authors an opportunity to reconsider their options.

In the worst case, excited authors sign away their rights in exchange for the promise of traditional publishing only to be asked for money to cover production costs later. This is a difficult situation, leaving authors with no right to publish their own work but without a published book.

The lesson here is to know who is offering you a contract. Look at what a publisher has done in the past. If the type of book a company publishes is random—a novel here, poetry there, political screeds interspersed with obscure spirituality tomes—proceed with caution.

While not a hard and fast rule, small publishers generally focus their efforts on one particular subject area. It's easier to market their products this way, and chances are good they have developed a devoted audience. Pure randomness may be a reflection of an individual publisher's tastes. Or it may be evidence that the publisher takes on anything as long as the author pays for the privilege.

If you are in doubt, search online for this publisher's authors, and ask them about their experiences. Also make sure that your contract has a date when the right to publish expires if a publisher does not hold up its end of the bargain.

CHAPTER SEVENTEEN

Publishing Path Five: Electronic Publishing

IN 2000, WHEN AUTHOR Stephen King published his novella *Riding the Bullet* in an electronic format—and made it the only way you could read it—the public chorus of "pooh-poohs" was vehement. The general harumph was something like "most people don't want to read their books on a computer."

Fast forward a decade and electronic sales of Stieg Larsson's *The Girl Who Kicked the Hornet's Nest* topped 775,000 downloads. At the same time, Amazon.com reported that the sales of electronic novels outpaced novels on paper.

Even if you are a devoted paper-and-ink person, I think it's wise to consider publishing your work electronically. Why not soak up as many sales as you can? This advice comes with some caveats, however.

The world of ebooks is changing while you read this sentence as the various ebook readers struggle to dominate the industry, and various electronic formats compete to become the default software. My advice at this point is to keep it simple. Stick your toe in the water, stay current on ebook technology developments, and adjust as companies such as Amazon and Google work to make ebook publishing easier and easier. It's in their financial best interest to do so. Remember, it wasn't that long ago that PCs and Macs could not open documents produced by the other. Nowadays, it doesn't matter what computer you use. My prediction is that sooner or later, the software used to run ebook readers will merge into a single platform used by all, and desktop publishing programs will have options that automatically convert documents into ebook-ready text. Then the real financial contest will be for distribution dominance—who will have the most books for the best price.

THE KEY CONCEPT YOU NEED TO UNDERSTAND

All ebook readers allow their users to individualize how text appears on their display screens. Some do this well. Some don't. The user of an ebook device can increase the size of text, change fonts, change its color as well as brighten or darken the background. In order to do this seamlessly, ebooks must be available in a format that expands, contracts, and reflows so text always fits the screen.

Given that most of us read text of some sort online, this capacity to contract, expand and reflow seems like part and parcel of everyday life. It is, but only because websites are constructed in a language called HTML (hypertext markup language) or a near relation. It's the presence of HTML coding that allows us to customize the content we read online. In order for this phenomenon to occur on an ebook reader, an electronic book needs to be in a form of HTML that meets the specifications of each individual brand of reader.

But—and you knew there was a "but" in here somewhere, didn't you?—the text on the pages of a paper book does not move. This means that the technical prowess necessary to make an electronic book is not the same as that needed for a book on paper.

Not too many years ago, book printers worked in a nightmare world of conflicting software applications that made it challenging to get a book to print correctly on paper. Then in the late 1990s, Adobe Systems released a little miracle into the technical universe, the Portable Document Format (PDF). In essence, PDFs became the language of the printing industry because they were not dependent on a particular software or type of computer. In other words, any printer— offset or digital—worked with documents in the PDF format.

But what works so well on paper is not the universal answer for electronic books. Why? At its most basic, a PDF is a set of instructions from which a computer can recreate a document or image. Think of a PDF like a map of Paris. A map can tell you a lot about Paris but it is not the same as being in the city itself.

This means that documents in a PDF format cannot reconfigure themselves to fit a screen. If you enlarge a PDF, the result is something like the large type sample below.

In order to read something in this larger size, you would have to use a scroll bar to move back and forth across the screen. Can you imagine doing that in order to read *Gone With the Wind*? Me neither. That's why the high-end publishers of ebooks have them converted into HTML code that's specific to each brand of electronic reader.

Yeah, it's one big confusing pain in the neck.

Now there are a number of companies that do this conver-

This is what text on a scree looks like when its size is in creased. The technology use in ebook readers automati- cally resizes text so that thi does not happen.

sion business for a fee or if you are familiar with HTML and are willing to learn the specifics for each type of reader, you can do this yourself. Personally, I like dealing directly with individuals when I buy author services so I'm going to recommend Rob Siders (www.52novels.com) as an addition to your list of ebook convertor resources. There are also websites that provide conversion programs that can be used on your own computer. Currently, Calibre is the most popular program in this arena (www.Calibre-ebook.com).

THE TOE-IN-THE-WATER EBOOK PUBLISHING PROGRAM

At this point in time, there are two principal ways for you to try ebook publishing without a large investment of time or money: Amazon's Kindle Direct Publishing program and Google Books.

Before you publish electronically, you must be certain you own the digital rights to your work. This means you have published your work independently or your book is officially out of print (if it was published traditionally), and all the rights to it have reverted back to you.

If you are uncertain about the status of a previously published book, contact its publisher.

If you have published your book with a self-publishing company, please read your contract carefully to be sure you own the right to publish electronically. Some companies do not take author's rights (Blurb and Lulu, for example) while others insist on all rights.

KINDLE DIRECT PUBLISHING

You can use a number of ebook readers to download books from Amazon.com's Kindle store. At the same time, Amazon has made it possible for anyone who owns Microsoft Word to upload their books for sale on the Kindle store. This type of publishing is called KDP, Kindle Direct Publishing.

TEXT VS. IMAGE

If your book is a novel, literary non-fiction, or a collection of essays or short stories, this is not a bad choice for your first independently published ebook. In other words, if your work is text with no images, I would try uploading your Microsoft Word file through the KDP program on Amazon.

YOUR COVER

If you hire a graphic designer to do your cover for you, be sure you ask to have that file converted into a number of different formats for use in print, attachment to emails, and on the web. At the same time, ask to have your front and back covers created as two separate files in the JPEG format. You will need these for ebook publishing.

PAY ATTENTION TO THE FORMATTING INSTRUCTIONS

Amazon is specific about the formatting commands you can use in Microsoft Word documents that you upload for sale in their Kindle store. Be sure to read and obey these instructions to avoid problems. If your book is not formatted correctly, the conversion to Kindle will not work.

ISBN

Always remember that a book's ISBN (International Standard Book Number) is assigned to the book's publisher, not its author. If you decide to publish through Kindle, do yourself a favor and purchase your own block of ISBNs. (See page 34 for more information about ISBNs.)

Currently, you can upload a Microsoft Word version of your book to Amazon's Kindle store for free. Also, if you price the book at $9.99 or less, you collect 70 percent of the sale price in royalties every time your book is downloaded. These funds are electronically deposited into your bank account of choice once a month.

GOOGLE BOOKS

Google is working to create the world's largest library, and putting your book in that library is another way to market and sell your work. In a nutshell, making your book available on Google Books works this way.

You can send Google a paper copy of your book. Google dismantles the book (which means they cut off its spine so never send your only copy because they don't send it back) then scans each page with a program known as OCR (Optical Character Reading). This essentially converts your book into a "live" version that can be searched.

Or you can upload a PDF version of your book directly to Google Books for free.

When a book goes live on the Google Books website, users can use the search engine for any term they choose. If your book includes a searched-for word or term—Episcopal, urban myth, Luddite, turtles—every book that contains that word or term pops up in the search results.

If someone clicks on your book, they can read a percentage of its pages. (The percentage is set by you.) These pages cannot be printed or saved or copied. Google has dismantled all of those functions except for books in the public domain.

If the reader wishes to purchase a copy of your book, Google provides ample links (including one to your own website if you wish) to places where folks can buy.

Both Google and Amazon provide lots of information about how to market your books on their sites, and enhance your book's position in its niche. My recommendation is to read these materials carefully, cull them for marketing ideas that fit your personal marketing program, and add them to your efforts. For more information about marketing, please turn to page 81.

CHAPTER EIGHTEEN

What's the Best Path for Your Book, Your Wallet and You?

SO NOW THAT you have all of this information at your fingertips, how do you know what publishing path is best for you? I agree that information is only part of the decision-making process, that a lot of how we make up our minds depends on our experience. And if you're just starting out on the road to publication, how would you have the experience to judge what will really work for you?

This lack of certainty, of anxiety in the face of choice is, in my opinion, what drives so many authors into the arms of companies that market themselves as "self-publishing." I'm going to be upfront with you here—except for a very narrow set of circumstances that I'll cover at the end of this chapter, I think these companies are a bad deal for writers because they give the illusion that all you need to do is write a check, and all of your publishing woes will vanish.

Except that this promise is not true. Yes, you can pay for good editing and good design. But the expensive (in my opinion) marketing services touted by self-publishing companies—email blasts, thousands of postcard mailings, radio services that make your voice "available" as an expert, advertising, and something called "expert positioning"—are no substitute for the genuine, in-person efforts of an author who's passionate about her work.

The same is true in traditional publishing.

Over more than five centuries, traditional publishers evolved a rather paternalistic view of authors. The unspoken premise became something along the lines of: "Don't worry, we'll take care of everything. We know best."

Because of this, writers as a group un-learned how to take care of themselves. As a group, we've imbibed the attitude that "writing" is something that takes place in a rarified atmosphere called art while publishing takes place in a foreign land that has nothing to do with us. Real writers, like British gentry in a Jane Austen novel, were never supposed to get their hands dirty with things like sales.

Personally, I think this is a false dichotomy. If a writer's work is not read, if it is not presented in a format that others can peruse and appreciate, the work of its author is incomplete. Publishing is a much a part of a writer's work as public performance is part of an actor's trade. Expecting someone else to care as much about your work as you do just doesn't cut it, no matter who's paying the bills.

So where does this leave you?

Remember at the beginning of this book, I asked you why you wanted to publish your work. That's where part of this answer lies, with you and your vision of yourself as a writer with a career to grow. In other words, how do you define success? And how do you assess your chances of attaining it?

I like stories so let me tell you about three very different, independently publishing authors, and how they succeeded.

First of all, you need to know that approximately 85 percent of all the books published in the U.S. are non-fiction. That huge category includes art books, biographies, spiritual and religious texts, philosophy, self-help, essay collections, how-to guides, business and finance, cookbooks, histories, literary non-fiction, and memoirs. Everything, in fact, except novels and short story collections.

Non-fiction, just by its very nature, is easier to market because it is easier to describe, easier to place in a niche, easier for readers to find. But that doesn't necessarily mean non-fiction authors have a better success rate than fiction authors. Unless you're someone like Eleanor Burns.

ELEANOR BURNS

If you're a quilter or even just interested in quilts, you've probably heard the name Eleanor Burns, or about her company, Quilt in a Day (www.QuiltinaDay.com), or seen her show of the same name on television. What you may not know is that Eleanor started her multi-million dollar company with an independently published book called *Make a Quilt in a Day—Log Cabin Pattern*.

That was in 1978. The first incarnation of her book was a set of typewritten and copied sheets of paper that Eleanor used in her classes to explain a new way of performing some common tasks in quilting. Her efforts could have stopped with those sheets except for one salient fact: Eleanor Burns is a gifted, enthusiastic teacher who uses her books—she's now independently published more than 100 titles—to share her passion for quilting.

In other words, her books are an extension of who Eleanor is and what she loves to do. This combination makes her a natural marketer, not because she has something to push but because she has something to share.

JUDY RINGER

Judy Ringer, author of *Unlikely Teachers*, has that same quality. Judy (www.JudyRinger.com) has a black belt in the martial art known as aikido. In aikido, a practitioner defends herself by redirecting the energy of an attacker rather than opposing it.

Judy utilizes this principle as a way of teaching others how to manage conflict in their lives and workplaces. Her book, which she independently published, grew out of her classes. Now when she teaches, her students can bring her lessons home with them. Like Eleanor Burns, Judy's passion for her work and her desire to share it with others makes her a natural marketer. Both women have successfully expanded their careers as teachers by adding books to what they offer their students. Judy printed her book via offset, sold all of her initial print run, and is now selling her second order of books.

TEACHING AND PUBLISHING

In my opinion, teaching and independent publishing are a dynamic combination because each effort promotes and expands on the other. Sometimes this relationship works in reverse, as in the case of the doctor I told you about on page 147. In that instance, publication led to speaking engagements, and opportunities to teach.

Why is this so? If you are an independent teacher like Eleanor Burns or Judy Ringer, you have already identified your niche—your market—before you write, even if you don't think of it in those terms. After your book is printed, these teaching opportunities become hand selling and marketing opportunities, a chance to share what you do with others.

And if you write before you teach? As I've pointed out before, book projects represent enormous investments of time and resources by their authors. Publishing a book in your field of interest raises your credibility and your profile automatically. This doesn't necessarily mean that invitations to speak will just flow in your direction. But your book will open doors that you can walk through.

Actor and writer Woody Allen once said that "Ninety percent of success is showing up." Publishing a book is the showing-up part. Walking through the doors that your book opens is the remaining ten percent.

So my advice to writers of non-fiction is to look around carefully. Who shares your passion? Where do you go to learn more about your chosen subject area? This is your tribe, your market, the folks who will appreciate your gifts more than anyone else. Write for them, and then share your enthusiasm with them. And remember, if you publish your books independently, you are making a longterm commitment to yourself and your career. This is a better predictor of success than anything else.

But what if you write novels or short stories. Are you out of luck? No, the same marketing rules apply—know your audience, share your passion—but their application often needs a different approach.

BILL SCHUBART

Bill Schubart (www.Schubart.com) is known in Vermont for his commitment to several high-profile nonprofits in the state, and as a commentator on Vermont Public Radio. So when he published his first book, *The Lamoille Stories*, he had a working familiarity with much of the state's media, and its bookstores.

The Lamoille Stories all take place in Vermont with a cast of characters that arc familiar to those of us who live here. This means Vermonters are Bill's natural audience so he structured his marketing in a bloom-where-you're-planted fashion. He spoke at local libraries, local bookstores, to local media. As a result, Bill sold more copies of *The Lamoille Stories* than most traditional publishers sell of their novels.

His efforts and his unceasing support for the people and places who helped him market his first book paid off when he independently published his second, more difficult, collection of stories called *Fat People*. Because of their good experience with *Lamoille*, readers were willing to take a chance on a book of stories about people for whom eating and food are a compulsion, and *Fat People* is selling well.

So what's the lesson here? Fiction writers, because of the more general nature of their work, need to think of their authorship more as a brand than a book. Everything you write and market builds on what you wrote and marketed last time. My advice here is to teach yourself how to market your work locally first. Seek out audiences wherever you find them—libraries, book discussion groups, PTA meetings, historical societies, high school classrooms, anywhere you can reach where folks will sit and listen to you read. Take notes, take names, and when you publish your second book, revisit these places. You are now a familiar name, a brand.

Or, if the thought of reading your work in public chills your blood, ferret out every book discussion group, blogger, or review website where folks can learn about your work. No matter how you do it, you have to show up to tell people about your book. No one else, no matter how much money you spend, will be able to do this as effectively as you.

JUDGE FOR YOURSELF

Based on my personal experience, I've come to believe that marketing acumen is as important as writing ability when it comes to succeeding as an author. Sooner or later, if you want to make part or all of your living this way, you must come to grips with the idea that it all comes down to sales.

Every reader buys books because they want to know something. It may be how to make more money or how to build a treehouse or how to think about God or to find out if Elizabeth Bennet and Fitzwilliam Darcy finally get together. When you share information about your work with others (marketing), you are helping them find answers (sales) in their quest for knowledge. You are filling a need, one that's so important, it changed the course of history.

So the final call is yours to make. Remember, publishing privately (Chapters Eleven and Twelve) is an honorable option, one I recommend if you want to learn the publishing ropes before you make a larger financial commitment. Or you can get a taste for the trade by designing your own book on a website such as Blurb.com or by launching your book eletron-ically through the Kindle store on Amazon.com.

Going through the process yourself will give you the confidence to push yourself to the next level.

CHAPTER NINETEEN

Ta Da!!!

AS PORKY PIG used to say "Th..tha...that's all folks!"

Except that it's not.

Not really.

Because you're at the beginning of an exciting journey in a wide-open, exciting time to be an author—or creative person of any kind, truth be told.

The era of the great gatekeepers has, to a large extent, ended. The great movie studio execs, the record companies that controlled music, and the book publishing conglomerates no longer have a monolithic hold over the creative lives of talented people. Now we can all create and sell or show off our works to one another without waiting to be picked by someone else for greatness.

If you have the initiative, you can publish and sell your own books. In other words, you can pick yourself.

But I know that the challenges can take your breath away, especially if you're venturing out for the first time. In addition to my own books, I guide other authors through the hills and valleys of publishing.

So I'm making you this offer: If you feel you could use some help, send me an email at Sonja@FullCirclePress.com. Tell me where you are and where you'd like to go. We'll talk.

Put "Ta Da!" in the subject line.

Yes, I'm certain you can do this.

How to Talk Like a Publisher: A Glossary of Terms

Parts of the Book

BACK MATTER

Every part of a book that comes after the main text is lumped together under the term back matter. Back matter can include but is not limited to: a bibliography, appendices, an index, reference material, explanatory or historical notes, the next few pages of an upcoming novel in a series, a page about the author.

BAR CODE

If you turn this book over to the back cover, you'll see a long number with a barcode underneath. In book publishing, this barcode represents the price and ISBN of the book. A barcode makes it much easier to inventory books and track sales.

BINDING

Binding refers to how the pages of a book are secured within its cover. Bindings can be sewn, stapled, glued or made of spirals of metal or plastic. See also page 169.

BLURB

Blurbs can appear on the front cover, back cover, or the first inside pages of a book. They are quotes written by established authors or authorities in a particular field, or segments of a favorable review.

BOOK BLOCK

All of the pages of a book—front matter, text and back matter—are collectively referred to as a book block. A cover is not part of a book block.

CIP DATA

CIP is an abbreviation for Cataloging-in-Publication. Some books have CIP data on their copyright pages, some do not. This cataloging information is created by the Library of Congress and is used by libraries to place a book in its proper category on a shelf.

COVER

In publishing, a cover refers collectively to the front cover, back cover, and spine of a book.

DUST JACKET

Heavy paper printed with the front, back, and spine of a book's cover plus some additional length (book flaps) folded over the outer edges of a book's front and back.

FRONT MATTER

All the parts of a book that occur before its main text are referred to collectively as front matter. Front matter includes but is not limited to: Half title page, title page, dedication, epigraph, introduction, preface, acknowledgements, table of contents, pages of blurbs, and the copyright page.

HARDCOVER

If a book's cover involves cardboard, it's a hardcover book. There are two types of hardcovers: Cloth-bound covered by a dust jacket, and paper-on-boards. A paper-on-boards cover (also sometimes called a self-cover) consists of a printed paper cover that's glued over a front, back and spine of cardboard that is then attached to a book block. A cloth-bound book's cover is created the same way as paper-on-boards with a coarse fabric with minimal printing substituted for the paper. Then the book's exterior is covered by a dust jacket.

ISBN

This is an abbreviation for International Standard Book Number. Every publisher has unique ISBNs assigned to it. This number is 13 digits long and encoded in it are the continent on which the book is published, its language, and the book's publisher. The last two digits of an ISBN differentiate the individual book within that publishing house. For a more thorough discussion of ISBNs, please turn to page 34.

PAGE

In a book, a page is considered a single printable surface. To be clear, a piece of paper has two printable surfaces so it is considered two pages.

PAGINATION

This is the order of pages in a book from the title page to the last page.

SOFTCOVER (ALSO REFERRED TO AS PAPERBACK)

If the cover of a book can be easily bent, it is a softcover book. The material used to print this type of cover varies from printer to printer, but generally it is heavy card stock.

SPINE

The part of a book's cover that encloses its binding.

Production Terms

In publishing, the term production refers to everything that happens to a book from the time a manuscript is finished by its author to when it is printed.

COVER DESIGN

All of the elements of a book's cover, from the image on the front to the colors in the background to the style of lettering are chosen by a designer. Cover design includes a technical understanding of the printing process—whether on paper or electronic—so that when the elements of a cover are in place, the final product meets expectations.

EDITING

Please see the chapter on Editing beginning on page 37 for a full definition of the three levels of editing, a history of this part of the book publishing process, and what you should look for in an editor.

FIRST PAGES

Once a manuscript is copyedited and all corrections are made, it is handed off to the person who applies the book's interior design specifications to the manuscript. The result, when printed on paper, is called first pages. This is the first time that an author's work looks like a "real book." For more information about interior design, please see Chapter Seven.

FORMATTING/TYPESETTING

The terms formatting and typesetting are used inter-changeably in publishing. This process involves applying design specifications to the text of a book so it appears on a page the way it appears in the final book.

INTERIOR DESIGN

If you chose a number of books at random and look at their pages, you notice that the way they are set up inside differs from one to another. Cookbooks have a particular look that's different from a novel or a how-to or a dictionary. The way a book looks inside is no accident. The text is deliberately designed to serve the purpose of the book. This process is called interior design.

IMAGES

Everything in a book that's not text is lumped together under the term images. An image can be a photograph, a map, or a drawing. For a more in-depth discussion of images, please see Chapter Six.

Printing Speak

From start to finish, everything in the book production process is calculated to match the specifications of a book's printer. Printing is a technical process and you could write a book on just this part of publishing. It's not necessary to know everything there is to know about printing but you should be familiar with these concepts.

BINDING

This term refers to the manner in which the pages of a book are held together. While there are a wide variety of ways to bind a book, these are the most common:

• Saddle stitching: books with a low-page count (generally 48 pages or under) are attached to one another and to their cover with staples.

• Perfect bound: the inside edges of the pages of a book are glued with a flexible adhesive to the cover's spine.

• Spiral bound: a generic term applied to bindings that use a coil of wire or plastic to keep the pages of a book together.

BLACK & WHITE

This term generally refers to the pages of a book and not its cover. As you may have guessed, it refers to the application of black ink on white or cream-colored paper.

BLEED

When ink, pigment, or toner is applied to paper, it cannot extend to the outer edges of a page because this is where the paper is held as it passes through a printer. But we've all seen books where the images go right up the outer edges of the paper. This effect is called a bleed, and it is achieved by printing slightly oversized images on larger-than-needed paper which is then cut to give the illusion that the ink was spread right to the edge of the paper. Bleeds generally add to the cost of a book.

COLOR

In general, book covers are all printed in color so the use of this term refers to what's on the inside of the book. Generally, printing in color costs three times per page what it costs to print in black and white.

DIGITAL PRINTING

Please see the definition of print-on-demand on page 30.

DIMENSIONS

This refers to the overall size of a book and is expressed as its width by its height. For example, the width of this book is five and a half inches and it is eight and a half inches high. When this appears in the book's Amazon listing or in the database used by bookstores, the dimensions appear as 5½ x 8½. Dimensions don't matter in electronic publishing.

GLOSSY

If you own an art book or a coffee-table book with photographs, chances are that the images were printed in ink using offset printing on shiny paper. This type of paper, which is called glossy in the printing trade, is often coated with clay to prevent ink absorption so that more of the color stays on the paper's surface.

GRAYSCALE

This is the term used to denote photographic images in black and white.

GUTTER

This refers to the part of a book's interior where the margins of each page come together in its spine.

OFFSET PRINTING

This is the standard way in which large quantities of books on paper are printed. The term offset refers to the way that an inked plate transfers image or text to a rubber blanket which, in turn, transfers an image or text to paper.

PDF (PORTABLE DOCUMENT FORMAT)

The PDF is an innovation introduced by Adobe Systems Incorporated and is now the standard representation of files used in document exchange.

The PDF was a great technical leap forward because a PDF created in one program on a particular type of computer can be transferred and opened by any other computer. Before the advent of the PDF, printers had to own and know how to operate every version of every publishing software for every type of computer. It was a lot like the mess that electronic publishing is in now.

Many of the software programs commonly used by the publishing industry such as Adobe's InDesign, Quark Xpress, and Microsoft Word can export a PDF file that is universally accepted by digital and offset printers.

PRINT RUN

This term refers to the number of copies a publisher prints of a book at one time. The extent of a print run is derived from two considerations: the per-copy cost of a book, and the number of copies a publisher believes will sell.

Per-copy costs are based on the financial investment a publisher makes in editing, design, typesetting, author advance, advertising, and marketing, plus the expense of printing a book. Generally, a publisher aims for a retail price that represents six or seven times the per-copy cost of a book. For example, if a book retails for $12, the per-copy cost of the book should be about $2.

The second part of the calculus has to do with the publisher's perception of a book's potential popularity among its kind. This perception is usually based on a publisher's experience with similar books.

Just to give you an idea of what a normal print run is within the industry, a first-time novel from a first-time author usually merits a print run of 2,500 to 3,000 copies. A how-to book in color that's expected to have a long shelf life would probably have a print run of 10,000 copies.

If a book is printed digitally, there is no need to calculate a print run since this type of book is printed as needed. When a copy of a digitally printed book is ordered, a copy is printed and shipped to the buyer. Digitally printed books can be ordered in any amount.

SETUP COSTS

No matter what printing process you use to produce a book, it takes time to create what a printer needs.

While most people think of printing as the whirr of inked drums pressing their letters and images onto paper, this part of the printing process is actually the quickest and least expensive part. The bulk of the time in printing is actually spent setting up images and text so that they look right when they are printed on paper.

Setup costs are the most significant portion of the expense of printing, not the ink and paper.

SIGNATURE

Books are not printed one page at a time. The pages of a book are often printed on large sheets of paper that are then folded and cut to the size needed in a book. In offset printing, generally, a single signature in a book is eight or sixteen pages. In digital printing, a signature is two, four or six pages.

The total number of pages in a book must be divisible by the number in a single signature. For example, each signature in this book is six pages, and the total number of pages in this book is 192, a number evenly divisible by six.

Business Concepts

Like every other industry, book publishing developed its own shorthand ways of conveying information, its own business dialect. These are some of the most important and ubiquitous terms.

ACQUISITION

In publishing, commercial houses don't buy a book from an author, they acquire the right to publish and sell it. Over the past twenty-or-so years, editors in the larger publishing companies have morphed into acquisitions editors, responsible for finding new works more than for working hands-on with a manuscript.

ADVANCE

When an author hits it big, the size of her or his advance is the most impressive part of the news. But the term advance is really shorthand for the phrase "advance on royalties."

In actuality, an author's advance is roughly equivalent to what a publisher believes the author's royalties could amount to over the lifetime of a book.

An advance is not a gift from a grateful publisher to an author. It is a financial acknowledgement of the potential earning power of a book.

In general, smaller publishers (those publishing 25 or fewer books per year) pay advances of $500 to $1,000 to their authors. Mid-sized publishers (26 to 100 books a year) pay up to $2,000 while large publishers pay $3,000 for a first-time novel, $5,000 to $8,000 for a non-fiction book.

The royalties that an author earns from the sales of his or her book are deducted from the amount of the advance until the advance is paid back to the publisher. Within the commercial publishing industry, more than 60 percent of all authors do not earn back their advances.

AGENTS (ALSO SOMETIMES CALLED REPS)

Agents have become the gatekeepers for the traditional publishing industry over the past 30 years. They have become the ones who decide what books are presented to acquisitions editors in the bigger establishments.

Their job is to present the work of an author to appropriate publishing outlets, and protect an author's rights during contract negotiations.

If a publisher decides to acquire an author's work, the author's agent receives 15 to 20 percent of the advance and 15 to 20 percent of any royalties for the lifetime of the book. Proceeds from the sale of a book are sent from the publisher to the agent who deducts her or his commission and then sends the remainder to the author. Nowadays, most publishing houses will not look at manuscripts unless they are presented by an agent.

It is important to consult a reputable attorney before signing any contract, and this applies to contracts between agents and authors.

AUTHOR DISCOUNT

When an author signs a contract with a traditional publisher, it generally includes a stipulation that the author will receive a certain number of books from the print run to sell or to give away as he or she wishes. There's usually an additional stipulation that authors can purchase more copies of their book at a certain discount off of the book's retail price. This author discount is generally 40 to 50 percent.

The one caveat is that the author cannot sell her or his own book to a bookseller (online as well as bricks-and-mortar) or library. Those sales are reserved for the publisher.

If you decide to seek a traditional publisher for your work, be sure your contract includes these clauses because it's important to have copies of your book to accompany your marketing efforts.

CATALOGING-IN-PUBLICATION (CIP)

Cataloging-in-publication data is a free service of the Library of Congress. There's an in-depth discussion of CIP on page 139 with more detail under the Library of Congress and Publishers Cataloging-in-Publication entries in this glossary.

CONTRACT

In book publishing, the contract between an author and a publishing company sets out what is expected from each party. Among its many stipulations, it usually covers:

- The amount of any advance and the author's royalty rates.

- When the completed manuscript is due from the author.

- What penalties authors face if they fail to live up to their part of the contract.

- What rights the publisher has to publish the author's work.

- In vanity publishing, a contract covers what the author agrees to pay for what work.

- Where authors can sell books and where they cannot.

- In what formats (print, web-based, electronic book) the author's work will be made available to the public.

- Sometimes an obligation by the author to submit any new works (usually limited to two) to the publisher before submitting them to someone else. This is often referred to as the right of first refusal.

- The name of the author's agent and that the agent is responsible for distributing any profits from sales of the book from the publisher to its author.

It is vitally important that you read every contract closely, and question everything you do not understand. Reputable agents can explain what the provisions of a publishing contract entail but do your own homework.

And please, if you decide to publish your work with a company that markets itself as a "self-publisher," be especially sure to have your contract vetted by a qualified copyright attorney. You can unknowingly sign away all the rights to your work forever with some of these contracts so you should proceed with caution.

An excellent source of information about the contracts offered by self-publishing companies is a book called *The Fine Print of Self-Publishing* by Mark Levine. And the Science Fiction & Fantasy Writers of America maintain a great website about the scams, schemes, and shams you can find in the publishing business at:

www.sfwa.org/for-authors/writer-beware.

COPYRIGHT

In the U.S. and many other countries throughout the world, a copyright is considered a property right exercised by the creator of an original work that is manifested in a tangible form. Copyrights for books in this country are established as soon as an author writes her or his work, and extend throughout an author's lifetime plus 75 years.

Before 1989, works had to be registered with a federal agency to be considered legally copyrighted, and they had to bear the © symbol. This is no longer true in the U.S. as well as in other countries who are signatories to the international copyright treaty created by the Berne Convention for the Protection of Literary and Artistic works. The original convention was held in 1886 and the stipulations of that agreement have been periodically renegotiated since.

You should know that registering your work does not give it any more protection legally than if you don't register it.

Because copyrights are property rights, their owners (in the case of books, the owner is the writer) have the right to sell licenses to reproduce their work. This is what happens when an author signs a contract with a publisher—the author is granting a license to the publisher to present his or her work in certain formats for sale to the public.

The term rights, defined later in this glossary, is a shortened version of the term copyright licenses. As always, you are urged to be cautious and seek professional advice any time you negotiate a contract.

One item worthy of note: many authors express a fear that their work will be stolen. The number of cases in the U.S. of stolen literary works (and that term covers fiction, poetry, essays and every form of non-fiction you can think of) are so few in number, it's really not worth talking about. If you come across someone trying to sell you copyright protection, check to make sure your wallet is still in your pocket, and then walk away.

COPYRIGHT PAGE

The copyright page of a book is actually the legal notice to the public about who owns the rights to a work and who has licensed those rights for publication. At a minimum, a copyright page should include: A book's full title (including subtitle), the author's name, the copyright notice (including the year) for the author including the © symbol, the book's publisher and location with the year of publication. The copyright page also includes any permission information such as who holds the copyright to a cover image or images used on the interior of a book, and the permission and copyright holders of any materials quoted within a book. It's not necessary but it is good information if you include the name of a book's designer and cover designer. If CIP data is avaiable (see the entry on page 173), it belongs at the bottom of the copyright page.

DISTRIBUTION

The short definition of the term distribution is the process of getting books from publishers to places where they can be

sold. In the U.S., the largest distributor of books and audiobooks is the Ingram Content Group. Nearly every independent bookstore and several online booksellers utilize the
Ingram database (which carries more than a million titles) to
locate and order books.

The second-largest distributor in the U.S. is Baker &
Taylor. While both companies serve the library market, Baker
& Taylor has a reputation for paying a lot of attention to the
needs of libraries.

In addition to Ingram and Baker & Taylor, there is a wide
variety of wholesalers that serve different speciality markets.
For example, books on quilting are distributed to fabric shops
by wholesalers such as Checker Distributors. The religious
market has its own distribution channels as do museums and
chain bookstores.

FRONTLIST/BACKLIST

In traditional publishing, there are two seasons during
which new books are introduced to the reading public. They
are Spring/Summer and Fall/Winter.

When a book debuts, it is part of what is called the front
list. In other words, it's new this season.

After that one season, books on the frontlist join all of the
publisher's older titles on what is called the backlist. Generally, this means that the publisher has a number of copies of
a book in its warehouse, and will continue to fulfill orders for
that book as long as there are sales enough to justify the
space the book takes up in the warehouse.

There's a wide difference of opinion among publishers
about how long to keep a title on a backlist, and when to put
a title out of print. Until the 1980s, most publishers kept
titles on their backlist forever, using sales from the backlist
to underwrite the cost of publishing new books. But changes
in tax laws governing inventory, and the rising costs of warehousing books changed some of this thinking. Nowadays,
most publishers maintain a minimum sales threshold, and

when a book's sales fall below that, the book is put out of print. (See definition below.)

HURTS

Books that are returned damaged to a publisher are generally referred to as "hurts." These books are often set aside to be sold to remainder dealers.

LIBRARY OF CONGRESS (LOC)

The Library of Congress provides free cataloging information to qualifying publishers for use on their copyright pages. In order to be eligible for LOC cataloging, a publisher must have published three books by different authors before it can apply for acceptance by the LOC. This standard was put in place years ago when self-publishing became popular in order to stem the flood of low-quality books into the LOC system.

If you are an independent publisher who doesn't qualify for cataloging by the Library of Congress, please see the entry under Publishers Cataloging-in-Publication in this glossary.

OUT OF PRINT/OP

Before the advent of digital book printing, a publisher put a book out of print under two conditions: They sold all existing copies of the book and did not plan to print more; sales of a book became too low to justify shelf space in the publisher's warehouse.

Under these circumstances, the right to publish a book reverted back to its author or the author's heirs. Unless an author made an effort to print copies of the book, it ceased to exist. Digital book printing changed this calculus.

Since a digitally-printed book exists only as a digital file until someone orders a copy of it, there is no need for a publisher to go to the expense of maintaining a warehouse to hold books. This means there is no reason not to keep a book in print indefinitely. And since there is no statute of limitations on a contract between an author and publisher, the

author may never regain control of her or his work.
Depending on the relationship between an author and
publisher, this may or may not present a problem.

PUBLISHERS CATALOGING-IN-PUBLICATION (PCIP)

If you decide to independently publish your book with
your own publishing company, and want cataloging information for your copyright page, you can hire a company called
Quality Books (www.Quality-Books.com) to provide what is
called Publishers Cataloging in Publication (PCIP) data. The
cost is $100 and the information is the same as that provided
by the Library of Congress.

Another choice is to find yourself a savvy librarian and
work with her or him to create cataloging info for your copyright page. As a rule, no librarian is really going to care where
your cataloging information came from. They just care if it's
accurate and useful.

PICK AND PACK

This term refers to the process of fulfilling orders of books
in a warehouse. People working in a book publisher's warehouse choose (pick) books that are ordered by a bookseller or
distributor then ship (pack) them.

Within the publishing universe, there is a constant
squabble over who pays for shipping costs. Generally it is the
publisher and not the bookseller.

REMAINDER

Remainders are the copies of a book left on a warehouse
shelf once the sales life of a book is over. Once sales drop
below a certain level—and this varies from publisher to
publisher—a book takes up space in a warehouse that's
needed for newer titles. Any remaining copies are sold to
specialized dealers for a small fraction of the book's retail
price, generally from $1 to $3 per copy. The dealers, in turn,
are free to sell the books for as much as the market will bear.

Only hardcover books are remaindered, and the copies are

marked—usually with a black felt-tipped marker along the edge of the pages—so they cannot be returned. Softcover books left over after a title's sales life are stripped of their covers and pulped.

Sometimes a publisher notifies an author that her or his book is going to be remaindered so the author can purchase copies of it.

RETAIL PRICE

The retail price of a book is the cost to the reader as it is set by a book's publisher. A bookseller may choose to offer a discount price on a book to encourage sales but the retail price is that originally set by the book's publisher.

In order to determine what you should charge for a retail price in independent publishing for books on paper, figure out your printing cost per copy. Then choose a reasonable retail price for your book (based on comparisons with others like it in the same niche), and deduct the standard trade discount from that price (55 percent of the full retail). Deduct the per-copy cost of printing from the remainder to determine how much of the retail price will be yours as the book's publisher.

Generally, a good retail price should leave an independent publisher with $2.50 to $3.00 per copy when copies are sold through a bookseller. Adjust your retail price until you reach this level.

RETURNABLE/RETURNS

Of all the issues in publishing, none is more controversial that the subject of returns.

In the traditional book publishing universe, bookstores have always been the primary market for publishers. During the Depression of the 1930s, the book publishing and book-selling industries were centered in New York City. Business was awful for everyone.

In an attempt to ease some of their financial pressures, a number of the larger booksellers asked their suppliers (publishers) for 90 days to pay for the books they ordered, and for the right to return any unsold inventory for full credit.

Publishers agreed to this, and this returns policy has been part and parcel of traditional publishing ever since.

From a publisher's point of view, this means that no book can be considered sold until 90 days have passed. It means that author royalties are paid 90 days after books are ordered, and the cost of returned books is deducted from those royalties. It is estimated (no one in publishing ever owns up to this number) that up to 70 percent of all books are returned by booksellers to traditional publishers.

It also means that booksellers will not order or stock copies of a book, no matter how it is published, unless the unsold copies are returnable.

In contrast, the returns on digitally printed books are generally very small, and returns on electronic books nil.

REVIEW COPY/ARC/GALLEY/UNCORRECTED PAGE PROOF

The whole idea behind book reviews is that they appear at approximately the same moment that a title is presented for sale to the public.

Of course, writing reviews takes time, and in places such as the *New York Times* or *Publishers Weekly* or *Booklist*, the turnaround time between receiving a book submitted for review and printing that review can be as long as six months. This is true even of online review publications.

Because publishers (and authors) consider reviews a critical component to marketing a new title, a number of ways of meeting the needs of reviewers have been devised.

Nowadays, pre-publication copies of hardcover books (the ones most likely to be reviewed) are printed digitally with a paper cover and the words "Advanced Reading Copy" (ARC) on the front and a list of marketing plans on the back.

For the larger review organizations, this marketing data is key because it shows how serious a publisher is about backing a book financially. Given the thousands of new titles published in the U.S. every year and the miniscule number that are reviewed, reviewers use this marketing information as a way to weed the "serious" books from the not-so-serious.

Over the years, review copies have gone by several names: folded-and-gathered sheets, Cranes (named for a company on Cape Cod that used to print review copies), galleys, and Uncorrected Page Proofs.

RIGHTS

Though we use the term "copyright" as a singular noun, a copyright is actually several different licensing rights, all of which can be sold by the author.

In book publishing, buying and selling rights can be a lucrative source of alternative income for publishers and authors.

The subject of rights is tricky, and can be a source of contention between a publisher and an author. Before the internet made publishing a global medium, an American publisher generally bought the license (right) to be the exclusive publisher of the author's work in the English language. Publication in other languages generally calls for separate licensing agreements.

When the web came along and the ability to publish books electronically followed, publishing contracts began to change to include licenses (rights) to manufacture an author's work electronically. Digital printing also changed the structure of rights because publishers can keep a book in print in perpetuity without having to warehouse it.

Audiobooks are a separate right, as are movie rights or the right to use a work as the basis for a play.

The whole point of a publishing contract is the stipulation of rights, and authors need to take great care when they sign a contract that all of their rights are clearly delineated. This is true whether you're signing an agreement with a traditional publisher or one who markets itself as a self-publisher. You can, inadvertently, sign away all the rights to your work if you are not careful.

ROYALTIES

Royalties are the portion of the retail price of a book that an author earns through sales. Generally, royalty rates are set out in an author's contract and may be paid on a sliding scale depending on the book's total sales.

In traditional publishing, royalty rates vary widely so it's difficult to pinpoint a figure and call it an average. Generally, an author can figure on earning a dollar or less per copy sold.

The issue of royalties is especially important when you consider having your work published by a self-publishing company. Since the most important market for these companies is a book's author, the royalty rate is not as important as the purchase price of copies of the book.

SALES/SPECIAL SALES

As American publishing developed into a mature industry in the latter part of the 19th century, the sales of its products (books) were made almost exclusively through bookstores and to libraries. As the industry grew, the term sales retained its allegiance to the relationship between traditional publishers and booksellers (now including online outlets such as Amazon), and it's still that way today. Generally, authors who publish with traditional publishers are not allowed to sell copies of their books to booksellers or to libraries.

The term "special sales" refers to non-bookstore sales made by publishers to chains such as Walmart or to book clubs. The books you see in spinners at the drugstore or the airport, at conferences, in museums and in gift shops are all considered special sales.

In spite of the fixation on bookstore sales, it's routinely acknowledged that sales outside bookstores (for many titles) exceed those in bookstores.

SHIPPING

Like returns, the cost of shipping can be contentious between booksellers and publishers (traditional and independent alike). Generally, the publisher bears the cost of shipping books to distributors and to bookselling outlets.

Of course, it doesn't cost anything to ship electronic books, a fact that is spurring sales of this type of book.

SLUSH PILE

Since the days of Gutenberg, there have always been more writers who want to have their books published than there are publishers willing to take them on. In fact, it didn't take long for printers (who were the original publishers) to realize that some writers were more popular than others, and that some books sold more than others. It's just a fact of publishing life.

The slush pile is the name for the place where publishers hold manuscripts until they can determine whether they are worth the risk of publication.

Before World War II and passage of the G.I. bill (officially called the Servicemen's Readjustment Act of 1944) and the corresponding expansion of higher education in the U.S., the number of unsolicited manuscripts (ones sent by authors to publishers without an explicit invitation) was relatively small. Editors could and did give just about everything at least a cursory reading, always on the lookout for a diamond in the rough.

As the height of slush piles grew, however, the expense of maintaining this service grew as well, and publishers abandoned this practice. Today, agents function as slush pile readers which is why most traditional publishers will not accept unagented books.

STANDARD TRADE DISCOUNT

As a book makes its way from its author to its reader, it passes through the publisher, a distributor, and then to the bookseller. The point of this chain is, of course, the sale of the book to its reader.

The money from this sale is divided among all of the parties involved, and those divisions are set by contract. Of the full retail price, 55 percent is divided between the distributor and the bookseller. This 55 percent is referred to as the "standard trade discount."

In other words, if the retail price of a book at a bookstore is $20, only $9 of it goes back to the publisher who, in turn, pays the author a portion in royalties. The remaining $11 is split between the distributor and the bookseller with the bulk going to the bookseller. It's how the bookseller pays for the heat, lights, shelving, rent, etc.

This discount is referred to as standard because it is just that, standard throughout the industry for books on paper.

The trade discount for electronic books is still anything but standard at this time but it seems to be settling somewhere around 30 percent. In other words, out of every electronic book sold, 30 percent stays with the bookseller and 70 percent is returned to the publisher and author.

WAREHOUSE

When books are printed using offset technology, the unsold copies need to be stored. Some publishers maintain their own warehouses for this purpose while other publishers use warehouses supplied by their distributors.

Warehouses are the physical centers for book distribution, the place where orders are picked off the shelves, packed, and shipped.

The elimination of warehouses and the expenses of maintaining them is one of the advantages of digital print technology and electronic books.

Index

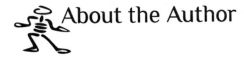About the Author

SONJA HAKALA IS the author of *Exposure: A Nellie Bly Mystery* (due in the summer of 2011), *Teach Yourself Visually Quilting, Visual Quick Tips Quilting,* and the editor of *American Patchwork.* She's lost count of the number of newspaper articles and magazine stories she's written. She's also worked with a number of traditional book publishers as an editor and project manager.

Along with her writing habit, Sonja is a book designer and professional quilter. In 1995, she founded Full Circle Publishing and Consulting Services to help authors find their way into publishing. Ten years later, her company morphed into Full Circle Press LLC. Through Full Circle Press, Sonja teaches other authors how to set up their own publishing companies and independently publish their books just as she did. Full Circle Press also provides author services such as editing, cover design, and interior design.

In 2011, Sonja founded the Parkinson's Quilt Project with the Parkinson's Center in Hanover, New Hampshire. The project's goal is to provide comforting quilts for people afflicted with Parkinson's disease.

Find out more about Sonja and her work at her website: www.SonjaHakala.com where she blogs regularly about writing, publishing, and other vagaries of life. You're welcome to email her any time at Sonja@FullCirclePress.com.

CPSIA information can be obtained at www.ICGtesting.com
Printed in the USA
LVOW041749130212

268491LV00004B/80/P

9 780979 004612